The Essence of
Financial Accounting

Second Edition

LESLIE CHADWICK MBA FCCA CertEc
Lecturer in Financial Management and Accounting
University of Bradford Management Centre

Prentice Hall
New York   London   Toronto   Sydney   Tokyo   Singapore
Madrid   Mexico City   Munich

First published 1991
This edition 1996 by
Prentice Hall
Campus 400, Maylands Avenue
Hemel Hempstead
Hertfordshire, HP2 7EZ

© Prentice Hall Europe, 1991, 1996

Typeset in 10/12pt Palatino
by Keyset Composition, Colchester

Printed and bound in Great Britain by
Bookcraft, Bath

Library of Congress Cataloging-in-Publication Data

Chadwick, Leslie, 1943–
    The essence of financial accounting / Leslie Chadwick. — 2nd ed.
        p.   cm. — (The Essence of management series)
    Includes bibliographical references and index.
    ISBN 0-13-356510-6
    1. Accounting.   I. Title.   II. Series
HF5635.C4385 1996
657—dc20   95-43148
                                                                CIP

British Library Cataloguing in Publication Data

A catalogue record for this book is available from
the British Library

ISBN 0-13-356510-6

---

8 7 6   5 4 3
05 04 03 02

Contents

Preface

Many of the managers and executives who attend short courses in accounting and finance, and students involved with non-professional accountancy courses, frequently comment that:

☐ They don't want to become accountants.

☐ They have no desire to become expert in the number crunching side of accountancy.

However, they do all appear to have a good idea about what they are really looking for. I have been told on numerous occasions by managers, executives and non-professional accountancy students that what they need to be able to do are the following:

☐ Acquire a good grasp of the terminology used.

☐ Understand how the figures which are produced have been arrived at, e.g. how the profit or loss for an accounting period has been calculated.

☐ Acquire a working knowledge of the important concepts, principles and techniques.

☐ Interpret and use the information which is generated.

☐ Know about the limitations of the information produced.

Who is this book for?

This book, one of the Prentice Hall *Essence of Management* series, has been especially written for those managers and executives attending short courses, either for reading before the course or during the course. However, students attending business and management courses of a longer duration should find the book helpful as pre-course reading or for reading during their course, e.g. it should be particularly useful for foundation level MBA courses or one semester undergraduate modules.

Why an essence series?

The books in this series attempt to get to the heart of the subject and explain the concepts and principles involved in a concise, user friendly manner. They have been developed to meet the needs of busy managers/executives attending short courses or those who wish to know more about the subject without having to wade through a mass of information.

What special features does this book have?

☐ Each chapter spells out the objectives which it is hoped will have been achieved by the time the study of the chapter has been completed.

☐ The essence of the subject is provided at the end of each chapter and is much more than a chapter summary.

☐ A number of self-assessment activities are provided, together with suggested answers and commentary.

☐ Many of the examples which illustrate financial accounting techniques take the reader through the process step by step.

☐ It uses a variety of techniques to put over its message, e.g. question and answer sections, diagrams, graphs and open learning.

☐ It has a user friendly approach.

1

An introduction to financial accounting

Objectives

The principal aim of this chapter is to introduce you to the world of financial accounting. When you have completed this chapter you should be able to do the following:

☐ Ascertain the needs of non-financial managers/executives/students regarding financial accounting.
☐ Understand why non-financial managers need to know more about financial accounting.
☐ Appreciate what financial accounting is concerned with.
☐ Identify the users of financial accounting information and why they need the information.

The quest for financial accounting knowledge

When asked what they want to know about financial accounting some non-financial managers are apt to provide an honest answer, such as:

☐ 'Nothing at all, unless I'm forced to.'
☐ 'The less I have to learn, the better.'

When asked why they wish to study financial accounting their replies may be equally frank, for example:

☐ 'It will look good on my c.v.'

☐ 'Employers tend to be impressed if you know something about accounting.'

However, the replies from other non-financial managers about what they would like to know about financial accounting are quite numerous, and really help to dictate the objectives of this book, for example:

☐ 'I want to be able to look at a set of accounts and understand them.'

☐ 'I want to be able to analyze, interpret and evaluate our financial performance.'

☐ 'I want to understand the principles which govern how we arrive at the profit or loss.'

☐ 'There's an awful lot of terminology and it would be useful if I could understand the key terms.'

☐ 'What is a balance sheet?'

☐ 'What is a trading and profit and loss account?'

☐ 'What is an income statement?'

☐ 'What does a statement of source and application of funds or cash flow statement tell us? Is this the same as a funds flow?'

☐ 'How is depreciation dealt with in the accounts?'

☐ 'Why are capital and reserves shown as liabilities in the balance sheet?'

☐ 'What are day books?'

☐ 'How does the accounting system work?'

☐ 'Where does all the information and data from which the accounts are prepared come from?'

☐ 'I'd like to be able to look at the published accounts and be able to compare them.'

☐ 'What are fixed assets?'

And so on.

Thus, the principal objective of this book is to respond to the needs of its users, i.e. non-financial managers and non-accounting students.

Which managers should study financial accounting?

In certain businesses each function may tend to keep itself to itself and their personnel are not encouraged to find out more about what goes on

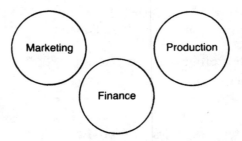

Figure 1.1 Business functions operating independently.

Figure 1.2 Business functions working together.

in the other functions. This is illustrated by Figure 1.1. However, in other businesses personnel are actively encouraged to find out more about the other functions and this is illustrated by Figure 1.2. This, it is hoped, will promote a better understanding of the other functions' activities and problems and promote mutual cooperation and coordination. Thus, marketing and production personnel need to know more about finance and each other, and finance needs to find out more about marketing and production. Individual business functions should not and cannot work in isolation because they are interdependent. They need to realize and appreciate that they are all on the same side and working towards the same objectives of the organization of which they are a part.

Financial accounting

To explain what financial accounting is all about we will look at a series of questions and answers.

Question: What is the end product of financial accounting?

Answer: The end product of financial accounting, frequently referred to as the final accounts, consists of the following:

☐ A trading and/or profit and loss account.
☐ A balance sheet.
☐ A cash flow statement.

In addition, various statistics are produced using accounting ratios, tabulations, graphs and charts. We will look at most of these areas in later chapters.

Question: From what source data are the final accounts prepared?
Answer: A multitude of source data, consisting of invoices, vouchers, credit notes, copy sales invoices, bank statements, etc. The original data not only provide some verification of a transaction, but may also be used to write up the books of account.

Question: How are the final accounts prepared?
Answer: The final accounts referred to above are arrived at by the application of the accounting concepts. The recording system uses a storage location called an account to record and accumulate details of a specific item of expenditure, for example the motor vehicles expenses account, or specific revenues received, for example the sales account. A separate account is kept for each item/group of items as dictated by the degree of analysis required.

   The accounting concepts are dealt with in the next chapter and a brief description of how the financial recording systems work will be covered in Chapter 3.

Question: For whom are they prepared?
Answer: There are many users/parties interested in the accounts of a company/organization. These include the following:

☐ The owners/shareholders.
☐ The directors/management.
☐ The creditors, i.e. suppliers of goods on credit.
☐ The investors, if it is a public limited company.
☐ The Customs and Excise in the United Kingdom.
☐ The tax authorities (the Inland Revenue in the United Kingdom).
☐ The Registrar of Companies, if it is a limited company.

Many of the sets of accounts which are prepared do tend to be drawn up with the tax authorities in mind, and this one factor may determine the figures which are produced.

Question: What do the users want the accounts for?
Answer: A variety of purposes, for example:

☐ The owners/shareholders use them to see if they are getting a satisfactory return on their investment, and to assess the financial health of their company/business.

☐ The directors/managers use them for making both internal and external comparisons in their attempts to evaluate performance. They may compare their own financial analysis of their company with industry figures in order to ascertain their company's strengths and weaknesses. Management are also concerned with ensuring that the money invested in the company/organization is generating an adequate return and that the company/organization is able to pay its debts and remain solvent.

☐ The creditors want to know if they are likely to get paid, and look particularly at liquidity, which is the ability of the company/organization to pay its debts as they become due.

☐ Prospective investors use them to assess whether or not to invest their money in the company/organization.

☐ The Customs and Excise and Inland Revenue in the United Kingdom use them for value added tax (VAT), and income and corporation tax purposes.

☐ The Registrar of Companies uses them to satisfy the legal obligations imposed by the Companies Act 1985/89. The Registrar of Companies will file the accounts and make them available for inspection as directed by the Act.

An introduction to financial accounting: The essence

Financial accounting is concerned with:

☐ The collection, filing and storage of financial data.
☐ The recording of business transactions in the books of account.
☐ The application of the accounting concepts.
☐ The preparation of the final accounts, which may consist of: a trading

and/or profit and loss account; a balance sheet; and a cash flow statement. These may be prepared for internal or external reporting purposes.

☐ The analysis and interpretation of financial accounts. This could involve comparisons with earlier years for the same company/organization and/or comparisons with other companies/organizations or with industry averages.

☐ In many instances, the management of the credit control function.

☐ The development of systems of internal control.

The non-financial manager and financial accounting

In today's complex and diverse business environment it is essential that all business functions cooperate, coordinate and communicate effectively with each other. Rather than working in isolation from each other, they should work together in harmony. This requires mutual trust and understanding and an appreciation of each other's point of view. This is why non-financial managers (and non-financial students) need to gain an appreciation of financial accounting. They want to be able to look at the financial information and understand it, use it, interpret it and be aware of its limitations.

The users of financial accounting information

There are numerous users of financial accounting information, many of whom are motivated by self interest, such as the directors, the managers, the shareholders, the creditors and would-be investors. Thus, a lot of time and effort is spent on financial analysis and the evaluation of performance.

Further reading

Berry, A., *Financial Accounting: An Introduction* (Chapman and Hall, 1993).
Pizzey, A., *Accounting and Finance: A Firm Foundation* (Cassell, 1994).
Watts, J., *Accounting in the Business Environment* (Pitman, 1995).

2

The concepts of financial accounting

Objectives

Having studied this chapter you should be able to do the following:

☐ Appreciate how the application of the various concepts affects the measurement of business income and the valuation of assets and liabilities.

☐ Understand the way in which the following concepts are applied:
- (a) money measurement;
- (b) realization;
- (c) conservatism (prudence);
- (d) materiality;
- (e) matching (accruals);
- (f) cost;
- (g) going concern;
- (h) entity;
- (i) consistency;
- (j) disclosure;
- (k) objectivity/fairness;
- (l) duality;
- (m) verifiability.

☐ Calculate the following:
- (a) the sales which would be recorded in the sales account for a specified period of time;
- (b) the expense for a period in which there is an accrual or a prepayment.

7

□ Know what the 'cut-off procedure' is, and what it is used for.

□ Understand why the application of the realization concept could lose you some money if you have to write off a debt as bad in a subsequent accounting period.

□ Appreciate that subjective judgement has to be exercised in order to apply certain concepts.

□ Know what is meant by expired and unexpired cost.

□ Understand what is meant by writing off a transaction as an expense, and carrying it forward as a balance.

□ Know which concept is responsible for the cautious image of accountants as perceived by non-accountants.

□ Give examples to illustrate the way in which materiality and the matching concept work.

Reread this chapter after you have studied Chapters 3 and 5 to consolidate your understanding and appreciation of this important subject.

It is not the intention of this chapter, or indeed the text as a whole, to go into any depth on the subject of accounting standards.

Accounting standards

FRS (Financial Reporting Standards) and SSAPs (Statements of Standard Accounting Practice) are frequently referred to as accounting standards and provide guidelines about a variety of accounting issues, e.g. taxation, cash flow statements (FRS 1) (funds flow), accounting policies, government grants, research and development expenditure, stocks and work-in-progress, etc. Although they are not legally enforceable, company accounts do tend to comply with them because if they did not the auditors would have to state this was the case in the auditors' report. There are also International Accountancy Standards (IASs) which have been designed to promote international harmonization.

The Companies Act 1985/89

The Companies Act stipulates many legal requirements which must be followed regarding the published accounts of companies, (see Chapter 10).

Financial accounting concepts

Many authors talk about accounting principles, postulates and concepts. We will simplify matters by calling them all concepts.

The concepts are the rules or guidelines which govern the way in which the figures are arrived at and stated in the final accounts. However, it must be mentioned at the outset that the application of many of the concepts does involve subjective judgement on the part of the person who is preparing the accounts. This means that two different people using the same source data could produce two entirely different sets of accounts! In addition to describing and illustrating the various concepts, we will also point out some of their drawbacks.

The money measurement concept

Only items which can be measured in monetary terms are included in the financial accounts which are prepared. This means that other more qualitative factors, which bring to the company/organization a high degree of success, such as management ability, morale and good industrial relations, are not included in trading, profit and loss accounts, balance sheets and cash flow statements, etc.

However, it must be remembered that money itself is not always so stable, for instance in times of rapidly rising inflation. The effects of inflation make comparisons from one year to another difficult, for example sales may have increased this year compared with last, but if inflation is taken into account there could, in fact, have been a decline in sales in real terms. Thus, in periods where there are significant increases in the rate of inflation, the financial accounts should be adjusted for inflation in an attempt to produce a realistic comparison.

The realization concept

This determines when we regard the goods or services which we supply as having been sold for the purpose of calculating the profit or loss. This calculation of the profit or loss is frequently referred to as 'the measurement of business income'. If goods are sold for cash, the date on which the cash is received is, for accounting purposes, the date of sale. However, with sales on credit, should we include the amount as a sale when the goods are despatched, when the goods are delivered, when the invoice is sent or when the customer pays for the goods? Figure 2.1 illustrates the cycle of the sale of goods on credit.

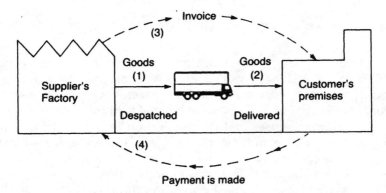

Figure 2.1 The sale of goods on credit.

Invoice				Invoice no. 007 5235
Nimwik Ltd				
VAT reg. no. XX4 3965				
Ref.	Quantity	Description	Tax point 4 Jan. 19X3	
			£	£

Figure 2.2 A VAT invoice.

Some texts say that the date on which the goods are delivered is the point in time at which the transaction should be included in the sales figure. However, in practice accounting systems do not include a transaction in the sales figure until the transaction has been invoiced. This is because there is frequently a time lag between the date on which the goods are delivered and the date on which the invoice is prepared and sent out, and the information contained on the invoice is used to write up the sales account. Thus, without the sales invoice the accounting records will not be written up. A useful guide to the actual date on which a transaction may be treated as a sale, for the purpose of computing the profit or loss for an accounting period in the United Kingdom, is the value added tax (VAT) point. Figure 2.2 illustrates a VAT invoice.

Thus, it can be observed that a transaction will be included in the sales figures when the goods have been delivered and invoiced, i.e. before the cash is received. Even though the cash has not been received, a transaction will be included in the sales figure for the purpose of measuring the income of a business, i.e. calculating the profit or loss.

We will now look at an example which illustrates how the realization concept works.

EXAMPLE 2.1   The calculation of sales for financial accounting purposes

Sales information for 11 June 19X7 was as follows:

	£000
Cash sales	12
Cash received from customers who had received goods on credit and were invoiced in April	17
Goods delivered to customers but not invoiced	21
Invoices sent to customers for goods which were delivered in May	43

The sales figure, i.e. the amount which would be included in the sales account for 11 June 19X7, would be as follows:

	£000
Cash sales	12
Credit sales (invoiced)	43
	55

The £17,000 would have been included in the sales figure in April, i.e. when they were invoiced, and the £21,000 representing goods delivered to customers but not invoiced will be included in sales when they are invoiced. However, it should be noted that some businesses send their invoice with the goods which are being delivered.

The realization concept means that for credit sales the *profit is being earned before the cash is received*. If a debt subsequently becomes bad and has to be written off, an adjustment will be made to the debtors figure for the period in which it is written off. This means that a business could pay tax on a profit arising from a sale in one period which becomes a bad debt in the next period. Tax relief will be available for the bad debt but there will be a time lag between paying the tax on the profit arising from the sale and receiving the relief for the bad debt. The example overleaf should help you to understand the financial implications.

If we take the tax paid for a credit sale in 19X3 and relieved as a bad debt in 19X4 as £40,000 and assume a one-year time lag between the two, and take interest rates into account at 10%, the cost of the realization concept to the company is £4,000. Therefore the company has lost the opportunity to earn 10% interest on the additional tax that it paid.

EXAMPLE 2.2   Bad debts and the realization concept

During 19X2 a sale was made to Upay & Co. Ltd amounting to £460,000. Tax was paid on the profits arising from this sale in 19X3. However, in 19X3 it was found that the debt was bad and it was written off. The tax relief for the bad debt reduced the amount of tax payable for 19X4.

Purchases
The purchases figure, i.e. the cost of raw materials for stock will include all those goods purchased within the period and taken into stock whether or not they have been paid for. So, here the key as to whether or not stock purchased is included in the purchases figure in the trading account is whether or not it has been taken into stock. This is why companies and organizations have to take great care with their treatment of stock which is delivered just before their year end. Many employ a special system for dealing with this called 'the cut-off procedure' which applies to both purchases of stock and sales. What does this mean? The cut-off is a date and any stock which arrives after that date is not taken into stock and is, therefore, not included in the purchases figure. Any stock which is sold after the cut-off date will be treated as a sale in the following year's accounts.

The operation of the 'cut-off procedure' does provide scope for 'creativity', but this is another story.

The conservatism (prudence) concept

The statements 'do not anticipate profits', and 'provide for all possible losses' illustrate the conservatism concept. The application of this concept means that the accounts tend to understate rather than overstate profits. It also helps to explain why accountants tend to have a conservative image.

The following are some examples of conservatism in action:

☐ Not taking any profit during the year on an uncompleted long-term contract where the final outcome is uncertain.

☐ Making a provision for bad debts. The profits are reduced by the amount of the provision, and the debtors (customers who have bought goods on credit and not yet paid for them) are reduced by the amount of the accumulated provision for bad debts in the balance sheet.

The materiality concept

The accounting treatment of many transactions will depend upon whether the amount in question is significant, and what is significant will depend upon who has to make that judgement. Let us take a look at how materiality may be applied.

A pencil may last more than one year but because its value is insignificant its cost would be charged in computing the profits or losses of the period in which it was purchased. Similarly, at its year end a company/organization could have a stock of stationery or advertising literature. If the value of this stock is adjudged to be significant, it will be carried forward to the next accounting period and charged as an expense in computing profits of that period, or the period in which it is finally consumed. If it is adjudged to be insignificant its cost will be charged in computing the profits or losses of the current period.

However, you must remember that what is significant will, to a great extent, depend upon the size of the undertaking. Items which are treated as significant by a small or medium-sized company could be treated as insignificant by a large or multinational company.

The matching (or accruals) concept

Subject to the operation of the materiality concept as described above, this concept attempts to charge to an accounting period only those expenses which are consumed during that period. We can in fact, for the purpose of matching, classify our costs into either **expired costs** or **unexpired costs**. Expired costs are those which are applicable to the current accounting period irrespective of whether or not they have been paid, and unexpired costs are those which have been incurred, whether or not they have been paid in the current accounting period, but which will not be consumed until a future accounting period. The portion of the expired costs which have not yet been paid is termed accruals or accrued expenses. Those expenses which have been paid during the current period, but relate to future accounting periods, are called prepayments or prepaid expenses.

Thus, the aim of matching is to include only those costs and revenues which are consumed or earned in the current accounting period, in the current accounting period's trading and profit and loss account. We will now take a look at some examples of the matching concept in action.

Stocks

Stocks of raw materials, work-in-progress and finished goods (if significant) held at the end of an accounting period have obviously not been consumed and will be carried forward to the next accounting period. They will be charged in computing profits during the period in which they are included in sales, i.e. matching the costs for the period with the revenue for the period.

Accrued expenses

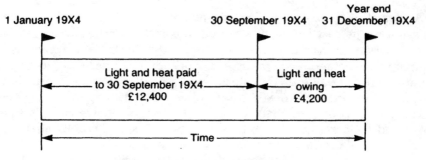

Figure 2.3 Accrued expenses.

Figure 2.3 illustrates accrued expenses. The amount which would be charged in the trading and profit and loss account in computing the profit or loss would be as follows:

	£
Paid to 30 September 19X4	12,400
Add Amount owing for 1 October to 31 December 19X4	4,200
Light and heat charge for the year =	£16,600

Also, in the accounts the amount owing of £4,200 would be carried forward and shown with other amounts owing in the balance sheet, under the heading of current liabilities.

Prepayments

If a company has paid the rent of £50,000 for its premises for the period 1 January 19X4 to 31 March 19X5, i.e. for 15 months, and the year end is 31 December 19X4, the company has paid one quarter's rent in advance. The figure which has to be included in the profit and loss account for the year ended 31 December 19X4 should be the rent applicable to 12 months, and would therefore be as follows:

	£
Amount paid for 15 months to 31 March 19X5	50,000
Less Amount paid in advance 3/15 × £50,000	10,000
Rent charge for the year =	£40,000

The £10,000 prepaid rent would also be carried forward to the next accounting period and would appear in the current year's balance sheet under the heading of current assets.

Some of the decisions which have to be made in this area are not always clear cut. Advertising which goes out and is paid for during the current period may also benefit the forthcoming period, for example advertising on television during late December to promote the January sales of retail establishments.

Once an accrual or prepayment has been carried forward to the next accounting period, it will have to be taken into account when computing the particular expense (or revenue) concerned of the next accounting period. This means that the calculation of an expense applicable to an accounting period will be as shown in the following example.

EXAMPLE 2.3 For an accrued expense

	£
Year 19X5 Light and heat	
Cash paid during the year covering the period 1 October 19X4 to	
30 September 19X5	17,800
Less Amount owing from last year (as per Figure 2.3) covering	
the period 1 October 19X4 to 31 December 19X4	4,200
	13,600
Add Amount owing for the current period, covering 1 October 19X5 to	
31 December 19X5	4,600
Light and heat charge for the year =	£18,200

The £4,600 for the amount owing for the current period would have to be picked up from the unpaid invoice, or if this is not available, it would have to be estimated when the accounts are being prepared.

You may ask the question why, after deducting the £4,200 was the figure of £13,600 greater than the £12,400 which was charged for the same period last year? The answer is simple – prices of light and heat have gone up by around 10%.

Depreciation

When a fixed asset is purchased such as equipment, fixtures and fittings, and plant and machinery, for use in the business and not for resale purposes, its cost will be spread over its estimated life. Thus, each year, as a portion of the fixed asset is in effect consumed, an amount estimated to cover that consumption, i.e. the expired cost, will be charged as

EXAMPLE 2.4 For a prepaid expense

	£
Year 19X5 Rent	
Amount prepaid covering the period 1 January 19X5 to 31 March 19X5	10,000
Add Amount paid during 19X5, covering the period 1 April 19X5 to	
31 March 19X6	46,000
	56,000
Less Amount prepaid, covering the period 1 January 19X6 to	
31 March 19X6 (1/4 × £46,000)	11,500
Rent charge for the year =	£44,500

an expense in the profit and loss account – this amount is called depreciation (or amortization). We will return to the subject of depreciation in Chapter 6.

The cost concept

The items shown in the accounts tend to be shown at their historic cost or historic cost less depreciation. This is because what we pay for an asset, such as equipment or stock, is a fact and all other values are highly subjective. However, the accounting standards which provide guidance on financial accounting matters do depart from the cost concept in certain instances, for example with the revaluation of fixed assets such as property, machinery and equipment, etc. and the valuation of stocks of raw materials, work-in-progress and finished goods.

The going concern concept

This states that the accounts should be prepared on the assumption that the business is going to continue and not on a winding-up basis. A winding-up basis would, in fact, place a lower value on the business and its assets.

The entity concept

The entity concept dictates that the personal and private transactions of the owner should be kept separate from the transactions of the business, the aim being to produce accounts for the business.

The consistency concept

If accounts are going to be of any use for comparability purposes, the figures should be arrived at using a consistent basis.

The disclosure concept

Changes which have a significant impact upon the accounts which are produced must be disclosed. Public and private limited companies have a legal obligation to disclose certain information in their published accounts, for example their accounting policies and significant changes. This concept tends to conflict with the consistency concept. The position could thus read – you must prepare your accounts using a consistent basis, but if you do change that basis, you are to declare it and disclose it!

The objectivity/fairness concept

Those who are charged with the task of preparing financial accounts should endeavour at all times to eliminate personal bias. However, because there are so many subjective judgements which must be made, this is not always possible.

The Companies Act 1985/89 requires that the published accounts of companies give a 'true and fair view' of the profit or loss and a true and fair view of the affairs as revealed by the balance sheet.

The duality concept

The duality concept refers to the double-entry bookkeeping system which is used to accumulate, in various accounts, the information from which the final accounts are prepared. Given time it is not too difficult to master. For example, if cash is used to pay an expense cash goes down and the accumulated amount spent on the expense goes up. If goods are sold on credit the accumulated sales figure goes up and the account of the customer who owes you the money, i.e. the debtor, also goes up. These are both examples of duality. Each transaction has a dual effect on the accounts. Nowadays computers can quite easily do the bookkeeping work.

The golden rule of double entry is that every debit should have a credit and vice versa. This will be explained in a little more depth when we look at the recording system in Chapter 3.

The verifiability concept

The accounts which are prepared should be capable of independent verification. Hence the need for auditors. We will review the role of the auditor in Chapter 10.

The above list of financial accounting concepts will, no doubt, vary from one 'authority' to another, but it should serve as a useful guide.

SELF-ASSESSMENT

Accounting concepts

Before looking at the essence of what has been covered in this chapter, see if you can answer the series of short questions on accounting concepts in the following self-assessment activity.

1 Which one factor can make it difficult to compare the monetary values of one year with the monetary values of another year?

2 The realization concept determines when goods sent on credit to customers are to be included in the sales figure for the purposes of computing the profit or loss for the accounting period. Which of the following tends to be used in practice to determine when to include a transaction in the sales figure (sales account) for the period:

when the goods have been

(a) despatched?
(b) delivered?
(c) invoiced?
(d) paid for?

3 From the data provided calculate the amount which would be included in the sales figure for August 19X8:

	£000
Cash sales for August	11
Cash from credit sales made in June and July	43
Credit sales for August:	
Delivered and invoiced	29
Delivered but not invoiced	8
Cash from credit sales made in August	5

4 If you include £96,000 for a consignment sent on credit to a customer in this year's sales and pay tax on it, and it then has to be written off as a bad debt in two years' time and you get tax relief on it, why has your company lost money?

5 What do companies/organizations use the 'cut-off procedure' for at their year end?

6 Which concept is based on the premise 'do not anticipate profits'/'provide for all losses'?

7 Which concept is being applied where an accountant decides to charge a year-end stock of correcting fluid, valued at £50, as an expense when computing profits rather than carrying it forward as an unexpired cost?

8 A business has a year end of 30 June in each year. You are provided with the following information relating to the business rent:

	£
Amount prepaid to 30 September 19X2 (covering period 1 July 19X2 to 30 September 19X2)	15,000
Amount paid for the six months to 31 March 19X3	30,000
Amount paid for the year to 31 March 19X4	72,000

Calculate the amount which should be charged as an expense for the year to 30 June 19X3 and highlight the amount prepaid and carried forward to the next year.

9 The annual rental payable for the use of business premises was set at £12,000. However, for the year just ended only £11,000 had been paid to the landlord. How much should be charged for rent in the year in question's profit and loss account?

10 Why is it important to adopt a consistent basis for the preparation of the final accounts of a company?

You will find the solutions, plus comments to this self-assessment progress activity, on pages 171–173.

The concepts of financial accounting: The essence

The concepts of financial accounting, appropriate accounting standards, and relevant company law are really the essence of financial accounting. They provide the rules, the principles and the conventions which govern the way in which the figures are prepared and published. They provide the guidelines for the measurement of business income, i.e. working out the profit or loss for an accounting period and the valuation of assets (items which the business owns) and liabilities (the amounts which the business owes). Several of these concepts have been incorporated into certain accounting standards and into company law. The concepts are, in fact, the foundation upon which much of financial accounting is based.

The principal concepts from a manager's point of view are the following:

☐ *Company law*
This relates to the accounts of limited companies.

☐ *Money measurement*
Only items which can be measured in monetary terms are shown in the accounts. Therefore, non-monetary items which are important to the success of the business, such as managerial calibre or good industrial relations, cannot be shown in the accounts.

☐ *Realization*
In the case of credit sales, the sale will be included in the figures which are used to calculate profit when the goods have been invoiced, not when the cash is received. Purchases are dealt with in a similar manner. They will be included in the purchases of the period if they have been taken into stock, whether or not they have been paid for.
  The cut-off procedure is a system designed to solve year-end problems regarding sales, purchases and stocks. If goods come in after the cut-off date they are excluded from stock and excluded from purchases. If goods go out after the cut-off date they will be excluded from the sales for the current period and treated as still being in stock, i.e. they will be treated as reducing the stock figure and being sales of the next accounting period.

☐ *Conservatism (prudence)*
This is the reason for the cautious approach followed by many accountants, as expressed in the statements 'do not anticipate profit' and 'provide for all possible losses'. This has the effect of understating profits and overstating losses!

☐ *Materiality*
The application of the materiality concept depends upon the judgement of the individual or group of individuals making the judgement, who have to decide on the accounting treatment of an item. The treatment will depend upon whether, in their opinion, the transaction is significant or insignificant. The size of the company/organization will no doubt influence the judgement.
  Thus, it can be seen from a study of Figure 2.4 that the concept of materiality is exercised to decide the destiny of a transaction, namely to 'write off' or to 'carry forward'. To write off means to charge the expense in computing the profit or loss for the current period. To carry forward means to treat all or some of the expenditure as unexpired and to carry it forward as a balance in the balance sheet to the next

Transaction adjudged to be:	Trading and profit and loss account (Income measurement)	Balance sheet (Asset valuation)
Significant	Exclude or write off a portion each year	Carried forward into the future as a balance
Insignificant	Write off, i.e. charge it all as one expense	Exclude, i.e. it has been written off

Figure 2.4 The effect of materiality on income measurement and asset valuation.

accounting period. If the item concerned is a fixed asset, such as equipment, fixtures and fittings or for research and development, we can describe this carrying forward process as *capitalizing* the expenditure.

However, you must also remember that materiality also applies to income, i.e. that which is insignificant and relates to the next accounting period could be included with the income of the current accounting period (notice the use of the word 'could'). The treatment depends upon the decision maker, i.e. the individual accountant concerned.

□ *Matching (or accruals)*
This concept aims to match the revenue earned in an accounting period with the expenditure incurred in earning that revenue. Thus, both costs and revenues are assigned to periods of time, i.e. the accounting period, for the purpose of computing the profit or loss for that period. This is why, at a company's year end, adjustments have to be made for accrued or prepaid expenditure and/or receipts, closing stocks of raw materials, fuels, work-in-progress and finished goods, and depreciation of fixed assets, etc.

□ *Cost*
Cost is a fact, i.e. the amount that was actually paid for the item in question. Therefore, the cost concept is used quite extensively as the principal value placed upon the transactions which are being recorded and reported. The accounting standards do, however, provide for alternative valuations in certain circumstances, e.g. the valuation of stocks or raw materials, work-in-progress and finished goods and the valuation of fixed assets.

□ *Going concern*
The accounts are prepared on the assumption that the business is going to continue and not on a winding-up basis which would value the assets

using their break-up values, i.e. what they would fetch if they had to be sold fairly quickly.

☐ *Entity*
The business should be accounted for as a separate entity and should exclude personal matters relating to the owners. However, with sole traders and partnerships it is not always possible to do this, so any personal expenditure is accumulated in a drawings account. With companies, great care has to be taken to ensure that the personal transactions of directors which go through their company's books are not treated as business expenses for the purpose of computing the profit or loss. If such expenditure were allowed to slip through, the accounts would not give a true and fair view and the company could be defrauding the tax authorities.

☐ *Consistency*
The accounting treatment of transactions should be the same within the current accounting period and from one accounting period to another. This makes for more valid comparisons of performance and promotes greater objectivity, i.e. those who prepare the accounts are not free to chop and change the way in which they arrive at the figures.

☐ *Disclosure*
Changes in accounting policies and other disclosures laid down by the Companies Act 1985/89 have to be reported. There is, in fact, a conflict between this concept and the concept of consistency. The disclosure concept is really implying that if you do decide to be inconsistent, e.g. changing your accounting policies, you must disclose it in your accounts. For example, an excerpt from some published accounts states: 'Had last year's profits been computed using our newly adopted accounting policy relating to the depreciation of fixed assets, last year's profits would have been £179,000 higher.'

☐ *Objectivity/fairness*
Personal bias should be avoided by those who are responsible for preparing the accounts. However, people are complex variables and their actions are subject to a wide degree of variability! The Companies Act 1985/89 stipulates that the published accounts of companies should give a true and fair view. This is referred to quite frequently as the overriding consideration.

☐ *Duality*
This concept refers to the dual aspect of each accounting transaction recorded using the double- (dual-) entry bookkeeping system. We will take a brief look at how this system works in Chapter 3.

□ *Verifiability*
The information generated by the financial accounting system should be capable of being verified by independent persons. Limited companies and certain other bodies are required by law to produce accounts audited by external firms of appropriately qualified accountants.

Finally, remember the following:

The financial accounting concepts, accounting standards and appropriate company law = **The essence of financial accounting**

It is recommended that you study this chapter again when you have completed working through Chapters 3, 4 and 5.

Further reading

Pizzey, A., *Accounting and Finance: A Firm Foundation* (Cassell, 1994).
Wood, F., *Business Accounting 1* (Pitman, 1993).

3

The recording system

Objectives

The principal aims of this chapter are that having worked through it you should be able to do the following:

☐ Appreciate where the data come from.
☐ Understand what cash books, day books (journals) and ledgers are used for.
☐ Understand how the double-entry bookkeeping system works, including the use of day books (journals).
☐ Construct an elementary control account for either the sales ledger or the purchases ledger.

Note that while this chapter is designed to give you an insight into the financial accounting recording system, it is not designed to show you how to become an expert bookkeeper. Figure 3.1 illustrates the components of the financial accounting system.

The data

The financial accounting system relies on a vast amount of source data. The accounting records which are kept may be written up from a combination of the following items:

☐ Invoices, credit notes and statements.

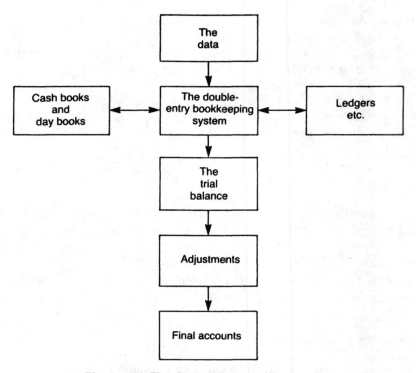

Figure 3.1 The financial accounting system.

- Banking records, e.g. paying-in books, bank statements, etc.
- Contracts.
- Payroll records.
- Stock records, etc.

Cash books, day books and ledgers

The financial accounting recording system uses various books of account. These books of account may be bound or loose leaf books, computer tapes or discs.

Cash books

The cash book is a book of first entry, i.e. the transaction first enters the recording system as an entry in the cash book. The cash book is usually used to record both cash and bank transactions and also the cash discount allowed to customers or received from suppliers. Many of the cash books that are kept are analyzed cash books, which means that in addition to recording money coming in and going out they provide a predetermined breakdown of the income and expenditure, e.g. an analysis of value added tax, purchases of raw materials, motor vehicle expenses, stationery, telephone, light and heat, etc.

A petty cash book may also be kept to record a variety of small cash payments, such as postage, cleaning materials and travelling expenses.

Day books

Day books (also called journals) are also books of first entry and tend to be kept for recording credit transactions. The following are examples:

☐ Sales day book, which records the credit sales.

☐ Purchases (or bought) day book, which records the credit purchases, e.g. raw materials.

☐ Sales returns day book.

☐ Purchases returns day book.

The operation of the day books will be explained in more detail later in this chapter when we look at double entry using day books. However, note that, as pointed out already, some writers refer to day books as journals, for example the sales day book can be called the sales journal.

Ledgers

The ledgers contain the numerous and various accounts which are used to store and accumulate the accounting information. Types of ledger include the following:

☐ *Nominal (or general) ledger*
The ledger in which the accounts are kept which are used to prepare the trading and profit and loss account and balance sheet, e.g. share capital, land and buildings, fixtures and fittings, sales, purchases, wages, motor expenses, etc.

☐ *Sales ledger*
The ledger in which the personal accounts record how much each credit customer, i.e. debtor, owes to the business.

□ *Purchases (or bought) ledger*
This ledger keeps a record of what the business owes to each supplier of goods on credit, i.e. the creditors.

Note that the above ledgers can be subdivided into a number of ledgers and that in practice other ledgers may also be used, for instance a *private ledger* which is used to record matters affecting the directors of a company.

Journals

In the United Kingdom journals may be used to record corrections of errors. However, many businesses/companies simply do not keep a journal.

The double-entry system

The dual effect of a business transaction is recorded by means of the double-entry bookkeeping system. Each individual account is used to accumulate and store the accounting information which is needed to produce the **final accounts**, namely the trading and profit and loss account, and the balance sheet. The way in which the double-entry system operates in the United Kingdom is to use the left-hand side of the account for debits and the right-hand side of the account for credits (see Figure 3.2). The double-entry system in the United States has the debits on the right-hand side and the credits on the left-hand side.

Accounting for cash and bank payments/receipts

A payment out of the bank would be recorded in the way shown in Figure 3.3. The effect of crediting the bank account with the £160,000 is to reduce the balance at the bank (or increase the overdraft). For money going out of the bank, the bank account is credited and the appropriate nominal (general) ledger account is debited, e.g. machinery account (as in Figure 3.3).

The treatment of receipts into the bank would be the other way round, i.e. the bank account would be debited with the amount and the appropriate nominal ledger account would be credited with the amount.

In practice, the cash account and the bank account will tend to be written

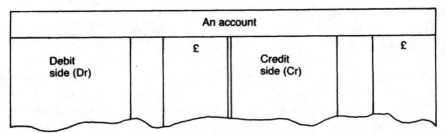

Figure 3.2 The double-entry system as operated in the United Kingdom.

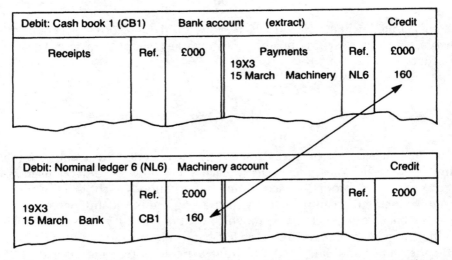

Figure 3.3 Double-entry accounting for cash and bank payments/receipts.

up on a daily basis, but the posting of the amounts to the appropriate individual nominal ledger accounts will be carried out periodically, e.g. weekly or monthly. This is why a cash book, i.e. the book in which the cash and bank accounts are kept, is called a book of first entry. The first entry for a cash/bank transaction is entered in the cash book, and then at some future date the double entry is completed when the transaction is posted to the appropriate nominal (general) ledger account.

Did you notice the operation of the cross-referencing system? In the bank account it states where the item was posted to, NL6 (i.e. nominal (general) ledger account number 6), and in the machinery account it states where the entry came from, CB1 (i.e. cash book, bank account, page 1).

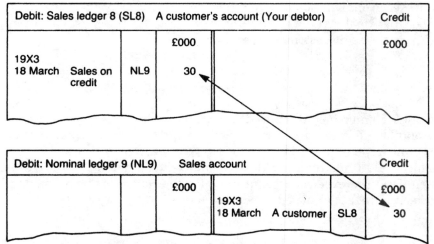

Figure 3.4 Double-entry accounting for credit transactions.

Accounting for credit transactions

The double-entry system also records the details of the buying and selling of goods/services on credit – an example of this is shown in Figure 3.4. For a sale on credit, the double-entry mechanism is to debit your debtor (i.e. your credit customer), and then to credit your sales account in the nominal (general) ledger.

For a purchase on credit, the double entry is the other way round, namely to credit your creditor (i.e. the supplier of the goods/services on credit), and then to debit the appropriate account, for example the purchases of raw materials account, in the nominal (general) ledger.

What happens when your debtors pay what they owe you? This is a cash transaction double entry. The cash received will be debited to the cash or bank account in the cash book and the account of the customer who sent the money will be credited, thus reducing or cancelling out their debt. Or, put another way, the cash or bank balance goes up or the overdraft is reduced (the effect of the debit), and the amount owing from the customer (i.e. the debtor) goes down.

The treatment of cash paid to creditors (i.e. suppliers of goods and services on credit) would be the other way round, i.e. the cash and bank balance would go down or the overdraft increase (a credit to the cash and bank account), and the amount owing to the creditor would be reduced (a debit to the credit supplier's account).

Did you notice that we tend to keep the accounts of credit customers (i.e. our debtors) in a sales ledger? This is because we need to know how much each individual customer owes us. This is why their accounts are called personal accounts and why we have to keep a personal record of what each credit customer owes.

Transfers

A double entry has to be used to transfer an amount from one account to another. For example, if we want to transfer an expense to another account we simply credit the expense account from which the transfer is being made (thus reducing this account by the amount transferred), and then debit the expense account to which the transfer is being made (this increases the accumulated expenses charged to this account).

A balance on an account

The balance on an account is the difference between the figures posted to each side of it, i.e. the difference between the total of the debit side and the total of the credit side, as shown in the following example.

EXAMPLE 3.1   A balance on an account

Debit		An account		Credit
		£000		£000
	Total	46	Total	7

	£000		
Total debits	46		
Less Total credits	7		
Net	£39	i.e. A debit balance of	£39,000

The trial balance

At the end of an accounting period all the accounts are balanced and the balances listed. Both sides of this list, called the trial balance, should balance. Because of the duality concept every debit should have a credit and vice versa, thus the trial balance is an arithmetic check that all the double entries have been completed. However, it will not detect errors such as the posting of a debit to the wrong account!

When the trial balance has been completed, some adjustments need to be made in order to comply with certain of the accounting concepts, for example the following:

□ prepayments;
□ accruals;
□ closing stocks;
□ depreciation;
□ proposed dividends;
□ transfers to reserves, etc.

The final accounts

The final accounts will then be prepared. The information needed for the trading and profit and loss account will be transferred from the ledger accounts to that account. All remaining ledger account balances will appear somewhere in the balance sheet, and will be carried forward as the opening balances to the next accounting period. A proof of these balances in the form of a trial balance, called a closing off, may be extracted to ensure that the balances carried forward in the ledgers and cash book to the next period are in balance.

Double-entry using day books

In cases where a business has a high level of purchases and/or sales on credit the day book system is to be commended. The personal accounts, which are kept in the sales ledger and purchases (bought) ledger for each individual customer or supplier, will have to be written up or updated for each transaction affecting them. However, the corresponding entry in the sales account and purchases account in the nominal (or general) ledger will be made using the periodic total of all the transactions, for instance on a weekly or monthly basis, as shown in Figure 3.5.

The treatment of credit sales using day books follows a similar pattern. However, you must remember that in practice a day book could be:

□ a file of invoices or copy invoices, or
□ a bound or loose leaf book, or
□ a computer tape or disc.

You may also find that similar systems exist for cash receipts and payments

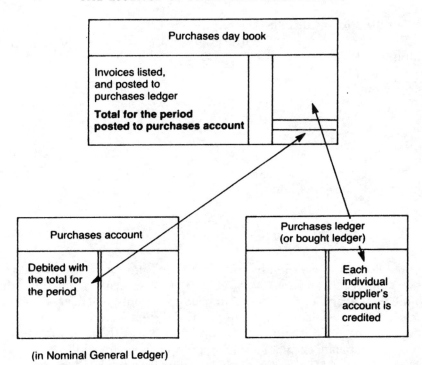

(in Nominal General Ledger)

Figure 3.5 Double-entry accounting using a purchases day book.

– the periodic totals being posted to the cash book and the transactions listed being posted to the appropriate ledger accounts, e.g. nominal ledger, purchases ledger and sales ledger.

Double-entry journal entries

Figure 3.6 illustrates how double entries can be made in journal form. You can see from this illustration that a journal entry used to describe a double entry consists of the following:

□ a debit;

□ a credit;

□ a narrative which describes the transaction/entry.

	Debit	Credit
Debit the cash account	£500	
Credit the sales account		£500
Goods sold for cash		

Figure 3.6 Double-entry journal entries.

Control accounts

A control account may be established to provide an arithmetic check on the accuracy of the balances contained within a ledger. The principle on which they work is quite easy to follow, and is explained in Figure 3.7.

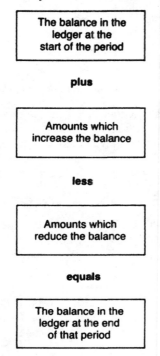

The balance in the
ledger at the
start of the period

plus

Amounts which
increase the balance

less

Amounts which
reduce the balance

equals

The balance in the
ledger at the end
of that period

Figure 3.7 The logic of the control account.

Let us now look at the following practical example.

EXAMPLE 3.2 Control accounts

The sales ledger balances at the beginning of the period amounted to a debit of £74,000. During the period cash was received from the debtors amounting to £42,000 and further sales were made on credit amounting to £58,000.

Sales ledger control account (Proof)

	£000
Opening balance brought forward	74
Add Credit sales for the period	58
	132
Less Cash received from debtors	42
Balance in sales ledger (i.e. debtors) at the end of the period	90

This illustration shows how control accounts are constructed. However, in practice there are other figures which will have to be taken into account, such as cash discounts for prompt payments, returns, allowances, etc. The treatment, however, is quite straightforward as they can only either reduce or increase the balance outstanding. Now see if you can complete the following self-assessment activity.

SELF-ASSESSMENT

You are provided with the following information:

1 January 19X5 purchases ledger balances (i.e. creditors) £78,000
During the month to 31 January 19X5:
Cash paid to creditors amounted to £37,000 and £3,000 discount for prompt payment was allowed
Goods bought on credit, invoiced at £4,000 were returned to suppliers (i.e. creditors)
Goods were bought on credit amounting to £25,000

Using the vertical mathematical approach, calculate the purchase ledger balances (i.e. creditors) at 31 January 19X5.

When you have attempted your calculation, compare it with the suggested solution on page 173.

The recording system: The essence

The data

The records are written up/updated using a variety of data, such as invoices, credit notes, statements, banking records, contracts, payroll records, stock records, etc.

The records

The records which are kept, frequently referred to as the books of account, consist of cash books, day books and ledgers.

Cash books contain details of the cash account and bank account. A cash book may contain details of cash discounts allowed to customers or received from suppliers, and may also include an analysis of the various receipts and payments.

Day books record credit transactions, such as the sales day book and the purchases (bought) day book, etc. Note that some writers call day books journals.

Ledgers are for storing details of income and expenditure, amounts owing to suppliers and amounts owing from customers, for example the following:

☐ A nominal (or general) ledger contains most of the information which is needed to prepare the trading and profit and loss account and the balance sheet.

☐ A sales ledger contains details of the personal accounts of credit customers (i.e. debtors). It is of prime importance that a business keeps a very good record of all those customers who owe it money.

☐ A purchases (or bought) ledger records how much the business owes to each of its suppliers of goods and services on credit, i.e. to the creditors.

Some of these books of account may be given other names in practice; for instance, the nominal ledger may be called a general ledger and may be divided up into a nominal ledger which excludes the accounts affecting directors, and a private ledger which is used to record all the transactions affecting the directors. The sales ledger may be called the debtors' ledger or receivables ledger, and the purchases ledger may be called the creditors' ledger or the payables ledger. The ledgers may also be subdivided, for example a company with a lot of credit sales may have several sales ledgers. The sales day book may be called the sales journal, and so on.

The records may be kept in bound or loose leaf books, on cards, on computer tapes and on computer discs. Therefore, when we talk about a cash book, day book or ledger, please remember that it could be stored on tape or disc within a computerized system. After all, an account is simply a storage location which is used to accumulate and store accounting information.

The double-entry system

The golden rule of double-entry is that every debit should have a credit, and every credit should have a debit.

The double-entry system is simply a recording system which records the dual effect of each business transaction. For example, if £2,000 cash is used to pay wages the cash account goes down by £2,000 and the wages account goes up by £2,000 (see Figure 3.8). If a customer is sold some goods for £15,000 and pays immediately by cheque the bank account goes up by £15,000 and the sales account goes up by £15,000 (see Figure 3.8). If raw

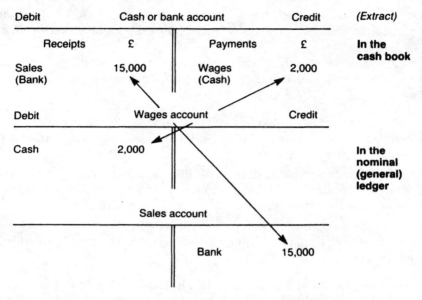

Figure 3.8 Double-entry for cash and bank transactions ('T' account format).

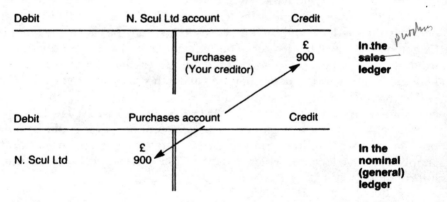

Figure 3.9 Double-entry for credit transactions ('T' account format).

materials are bought on credit from N. Scul Ltd for £900, the purchases of raw materials account will go up by £900, and the account of N. Scul Ltd will go up by £900 (a credit sale would have a vice-versa effect) (see Figure 3.9).

From Figure 3.8 we can see that for cash or bank receipts the double entry is debit the cash or bank account, and credit the appropriate ledger account. And for payments the double entry is credit the cash or bank account, and debit the appropriate ledger account.

The treatment of credit transactions, as described in the N. Scul Ltd example, is illustrated in Figure 3.9. The rule here is credit your creditor, i.e. N. Scul Ltd, with £900 in the purchases ledger, and debit the purchases account by £900 in the nominal ledger.

For sales on credit the rule is debit your debtor, i.e. your credit customer's own personal account, with the amount in the sales ledger, and credit the sales account with the amount in the nominal ledger.

The trial balance

This is simply a list of all the balances on the accounts. It is taken out immediately before the trading and profit and loss account and the balance sheet are prepared, the aim being to ensure that everything is in balance before the next stage commences. It will show up errors where a debit has been posted as a credit or a credit has been posted as a debit, or where the amount posted to and recorded in one account is incorrect. It cannot detect postings to the wrong account, for instance £500 which should have been debited to F. Smith and Co. Ltd being debited to J. Smith and Sons Ltd.

How can we remember which items go into a trial balance? All you have to do is remember Alice! ALICE being the first letters of the keywords in our illustrative trial balance which is shown in Figure 3.10. We will include more about this in the next two chapters when we look at the preparation of the trading and profit and loss account and the balance sheet, i.e. the final accounts.

The adjustments and the final accounts

Having prepared a trial balance and identified any errors, the next stage in the preparation of the final accounts is to deal with adjustments for accrued and/or prepaid items, closing stocks, depreciation, proposed dividends and transfers to reserves, etc. The final accounts will then be prepared. To ensure that the balances carried forward to the next accounting period in the cash book and ledgers are correct another trial balance may be taken out, called a closing off.

Double-entry using day books

A day book could be either of the following:

☐ A file of purchase invoices or copy sales invoices.

Trial balance as at 31 December 19X6		
ALICE	Debit	Credit
	£000	£000
Assets, e.g. machinery, fixtures, debtors, etc.	1,200 (A)	
Liabilities, e.g. creditors, loans		100 (L)
Income, e.g. sales, rent received		400 (I)
Capital and reserves, e.g. share capital, retained earnings (profit and loss account balance)		1,000 (C)
Expenditure, e.g. purchases, wages, etc.	300 (E)	
	1,500	1,500

Figure 3.10 The trial balance and ALICE.

□ A list of purchase invoices or copy sales invoices kept in a bound or loose leaf book or on a computer tape or disc.

An example is the sales day book in which the copy sales invoices would be listed and totalled for the period, i.e. weekly or monthly. The total would be credited to the sales account in the nominal (general) ledger, and the individual customer accounts, which are kept in the sales ledger, would be debited (i.e. debit your debtor). This means that the sales account is not overburdened with superfluous information.

Control accounts

Control (or total) accounts can be used to prove the arithmetic accuracy of the balances within a ledger, for example the sales ledger control account balance should be equal to the list of balances (i.e. debtors) extracted from the sales ledger.

Finally, before going on to study the next chapter, turn back to Figure 3.1 which details the components and processes within the financial accounting system, and see if you can understand it more fully.

Further reading

Langley, F. P. and Hardern, G. S., *Introduction to Accounting for Business Studies* (Butterworths, 1994).

Wood, F., *Business Accounting 1* (Pitman, 1993).

4

The trading and profit and loss account

Objectives

When you have worked through all the material contained in this chapter, you should be able to do the following:

☐ Calculate the:
  - (a) cost of sales;
  - (b) gross profit;
  - (c) net profit;
  - (d) retained profit (profit and loss account balance) carried forward.

☐ Have a good working knowledge of the format and purpose of the trading account, profit and loss account and the appropriation account, as used by a company for internal accounting purposes.

The trading and profit and loss account

This can be described in simple terms as the account in which the profit or loss for the accounting period is computed. A longer, more comprehensive description is the account which is concerned with the measurement of business income for an accounting period, for example one year. The economic activity of the accounting period is measured according to the rules, such as accounting concepts, accounting standards and the relevant legislation. It provides the answer to the questions 'how much have I made?' or 'how much has the company made?'.

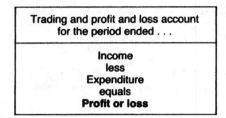

Figure 4.1 The calculation of the profit or loss.

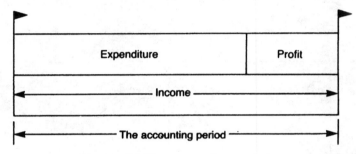

Figure 4.2 The accounting period.

You have probably encountered a type of trading and profit and loss account in your social life. The income and expenditure account used by clubs and non-profit-making societies is really a trading and profit and loss account under another name. The illustration in Figure 4.1 could have been called an income and expenditure account. If that were the case, the profit would probably be described as a surplus and a loss would be described as a deficiency.

The trading and profit and loss account is often **referred to as the profit and loss account (the P&L) or the income statement**. Thus, the income for the period has to be compared with, or matched against, the expenditure for that period involved in generating the income. This provides the profit figure, as illustrated in Figure 4.2.

However, for limited companies the picture is a little more complex. They produce an additional section to the profit and loss account called a profit and loss appropriation account (or the appropriation account). They also have to produce accounts for internal and external reporting purposes. For the time being we will concern ourselves with their internal accounts, as illustrated by Figure 4.3. The external accounts (i.e. the published accounts) of limited companies will be examined in Chapter 10.

The appropriation account shows how the profit for the period is shared up between the following items:

□ taxation;

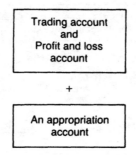

Figure 4.3 Internal company accounts – income measurement.

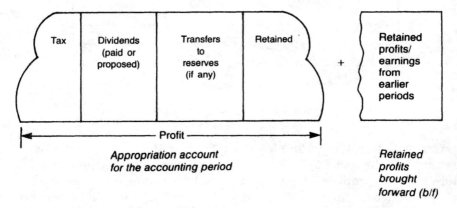

Figure 4.4 The appropriation account of a limited company.

□ dividends;

□ transfers to reserves;

□ retained profits/earnings.

From our 'loaf of bread' diagram (Figure 4.4) you can see that after dividing the profit for the period between tax, dividends for shareholders and transfers to reserves, the final portion remaining represents the retained earnings which will be added to the retained earnings brought forward from earlier periods. The cumulative figure for these retained earnings, i.e. ploughed back profits, will be shown as a reserve in the balance sheet. We will describe reserves and retained earnings in more detail in the next chapter.

We will now take a look at the component parts of Figure 4.3 in greater depth – Figure 4.5 deals with the trading account. The sales figure represents the income generated by the trading activities. The cost of sales figure is the cost price of the goods or services which have been sold during

```
Trading account
     Sales
      less
  Cost of sales
     equals
  Gross profit
```

Figure 4.5 The trading account.

the period. Thus, the calculation of the cost of sales will depend upon the type of product or service which is being marketed, be it retailing, manufacturing, or a service, etc. The cost of sales in terms of materials can be computed as shown in Example 4.1.

If the business concerned was involved in manufacturing, then manufacturing wages and associated overheads would be included in the cost of sales figure. The costs of production, i.e. materials consumed, manufacturing labour and factory overheads, would be calculated in a manufacturing account. This information would then be used in the trading account, as shown in Example 4.2.

In a manufacturing environment, the stocks of raw materials and work-in-progress would be dealt with in the manufacturing account.

The purpose of the trading account is to compute the gross profit, which can also be referred to as the gross margin, the margin or the mark-up.

EXAMPLE 4.1 The cost of sales

	Abbreviated to:
Opening stock of materials	Opening stock
Add Materials purchased during the period	*Add* Purchases
Less The closing stock of materials	*Less* Closing stock
= Cost price of goods sold	= Cost of sales

EXAMPLE 4.2 The costs of production

Opening stock of finished goods
Add Factory cost of production for the period
Less Closing stock of finished goods

= Cost of sales

Profit and loss account
Gross profit plus Other income less Expenses equals **Net profit or loss**

Figure 4.6 The profit and loss account.

	Profit and loss appropriation account
	Net profit (per the profit and loss account) *Less* Tax
equals	Net profit (loss) after tax *Less* dividends and transfers to reserves
equals	Retained profits (loss) for the current period *Add* Retained profits brought forward from last year
equals	Retained profits (P&L account balance) carried forward to next year

Figure 4.7 The profit and loss appropriation account.

The purpose of the profit and loss account is to compute the net profit or loss for the period, and this is illustrated by Figure 4.6.

The other income, i.e. the non-trading income which is added to the gross profit, could consist of items such as rent received, discounts received for prompt payment of amounts owing, investment income, etc.

The expenses could be grouped into administration expenses, selling expenses and distribution expenses. The expenses would include the wages and salaries of employees and directors (other than those which were dealt with in the trading/manufacturing accounts), loan interest and debenture interest paid, various overhead expenses and the depreciation for the period charged for the use of fixed assets such as plant, machinery, fixtures, fittings, motor vehicles, etc. All the expenses which are not dealt with in the trading/manufacturing account and appropriation account are dealt with in the profit and loss account.

The first calculation in Figure 4.7 simply states that net profit less tax equals the net profit after tax. From this figure the appropriations are deducted and could consist of the following:

☐ transfers to reserves, and/or
☐ dividends for the period which have been paid or proposed on ordinary shares (and, if any, preference shares).

When produced in statement form the three component parts of the trading and profit and loss account, as illustrated in Figures 4.5, 4.6 and 4.7 tend to merge with each other. We will now look at a typical trading and profit and loss account, as set out in Figure 4.8. While working through it, note the following:

☐ Layout and presentation are important.
☐ Key figures are highlighted, e.g. sales, cost of sales, gross profit, net profit, etc.
☐ Directors' fees, loan interest and debenture interest are regarded as charges against income and are therefore included in the profit and loss section of the statement. They are **not** treated as appropriations of profit.
☐ The appropriation section shows how the profit earned is shared between the stakeholders, e.g. the tax authorities, the shareholders and the amount ploughed back by the company, i.e. reserves and retained earnings (P&L account balance).

Having studied Figure 4.8 and referring back to it as and when necessary, now see if you can complete the following self-assessment activity to ensure that you understand what we have covered in this chapter so far.

SELF-ASSESSMENT

The trading and profit and loss account

1 Which two words describe the period of time covered by the trading and profit and loss account?

2 What name is usually given to the profit and loss account produced for a club or non-profit-making organization?

3 Which rules dictate/advise on how business income (i.e. the profit or loss) should be measured?

Scotgate Ltd

Trading and profit and loss account
for the year ended 30 June 19X4
(for internal use)

	£000	£000
Sales		250
Less **Cost of sales**		
Opening stock	14	
Add Purchases	165	
	179	
Less Closing stock	29	150
Gross profit		100
Add Rent received		13
		113
Less **Expenses**		
Salaries and wages	22	
Directors' fees	23	
Motor expenses	10	
Light and heat	6	
Stationery and telephone	4	
Rent and rates	8	
Loan interest and charges	5	
Repairs and renewals	7	
Sundries	2	
Audit and accountancy	1	
Depreciation:		
Motor vehicles	6	
Equipment	3	97
Net profit		16
Less Corporation tax		3
Net profit after tax		13

	£000	
Transfer to general reserve	Nil	
Ordinary share dividend paid and proposed	4	4
Retained earnings (for the year ended 30 June 19X4)		9
Add Retained earnings (i.e. P&L balance) b/f		27
Retained earnings c/f		36

Figure 4.8 A typical trading and profit and loss account.

4 Which one of the following statements do you consider to be correct? The appropriation account of a limited company deals with:

(a) Tax, dividends, transfers to reserves, retained earnings.

(b) Tax, dividends, directors' fees, transfers to reserves.

(c) Tax, dividends, debenture interest, retained earnings.

(d) Tax, dividends, directors' fees, debenture interest.

5 From the following information calculate the cost of sales and the gross profit:

	Opening stock	Closing stock	Purchases	Sales
	£000	£000	£000	£000
Materials	12	18	100	150

6 Which account would be used to compute the factory cost of production?

7 From the data provided, see if you can work out the net profit before tax:

	£000
Gross profit	184
Expenses	63
Depreciation	18
Dividends paid	6
Loan interest	4
Directors' fees	24
Tax	9
Proposed dividends	8

8 What other terms are used to describe the gross profit?

9 Calculate the retained profit figure which will be carried forward to the next accounting period from the following information:

	£000
Net profit before tax	114
Taxation	32
Dividends paid	8
Dividends proposed	10
Retained earnings b/f	38
Directors' fees	26
Loan interest	14

10 What other description did we use for retained profits/retained earnings?

You will find the answers to these self-assessment questions on pages 173–175.

The connection with the recording system

How does the trading and profit and loss account tie up with the double-entry system? You will recall that the recording system stores and accumulates the financial information which is needed to produce the final accounts. In the United Kingdom the expenses are recorded in the ledger accounts as debits and income is recorded as a credit.

Section	Format	Purpose
Trading account	Sales *Less* Cost of sales* equals **Gross profit**	To calculate the gross profit

Profit and loss account	Gross profit
	Plus Other income
	    (if any)
	Less Expenses
	    (including directors' fees,
	    loan interest, debenture
	    interest and depreciation)
	    equals
	Net profit (or loss)
		To calculate the net profit
		(or loss)

Appropriation account
 	
(See also
Figures 4.4
and 4.7)
	Net profit (or loss) before tax
	Less Tax, transfers to reserves
	    and dividends
	Add Retained earnings
	    brought forward (b/f)
	    equals
	Retained earnings c/f
		To show how the net profit (or loss) before tax for the period is distributed between taxation, dividends and retentions and to calculate the retained earnings carried forward

*The cost of sales calculation in its simplest form is: opening stock *add* purchases *less* closing stock.

Figure 4.9 The form and purpose of an internal company trading and profit and loss account.

The trading and profit and loss account: The essence

The trading and profit and loss account is the financial statement which attempts to measure the economic activity/business income of an accounting period in accordance with accepted accounting concepts, accounting standards and relevant legislation, etc.

The internal trading and profit and loss account of a company consists of three sections and this is illustrated in Figure 4.9.

It should be noted that directors' fees, loan interest, debenture interest and depreciation are used to calculate the net profit or loss in the profit and loss account. They are not appropriations of profit, but charges which should be deducted in measuring the profit. Also, note that the dividends which have to be included in the appropriation account are the dividends which have been paid or proposed for the accounting period which is under review. Note also, that the trading and profit and loss account can also be called the profit and loss account or the P&L, or the income statement.

Finally, an example of the trading and profit and loss account of a company (for internal purposes) was illustrated by Figure 4.8 for Scotgate Ltd. For an example of profit and loss format please review the example on page 198.

Further reading

Dyson, J., *Accounting for Non-Accounting Students* (Pitman, 1994).
Wood, F., *Business Accounting 1* (Pitman, 1993).

5

The balance sheet

Objectives

The aim of this chapter is simply to ensure that you become familiar with the language of balance sheets, i.e. the terminology which is used to describe the various constituent parts. Therefore, having worked carefully through the chapter you should know what is meant by the following:

- □ The balance sheet equation.
- □ Capital employed.
- □ Share capital.
- □ Authorized share capital.
- □ Ordinary shares.
- □ Calls.
- □ Preference shares.
- □ Share premium.
- □ Capital reserves.
- □ Revenue reserves.
- □ Long-term debt.
- □ The employment of capital.
- □ Fixed assets.
- □ Investments.
- □ Working capital.
- □ Current assets, e.g. stock, debtors, prepayments, bank, cash.

☐ Current liabilities, e.g. creditors, accruals, taxation, proposed dividends.

☐ Window dressing.

You should also appreciate the following:

☐ That the book value of an asset can be significantly different from its real value.

☐ How the balance sheet is affected by the cost concept and the money measurement concept.

☐ Why capital is shown alongside the liabilities.

☐ The characteristics of ordinary shares and preference shares.

☐ The limitations of the balance sheet.

What is a balance sheet?

In order to answer this question fully, we also need to specify what a balance sheet is not, and to identify its limitations.

A balance sheet is a statement of the financial position, in terms of the capital, assets and liabilities, of a business entity. It is not an account and not part of the double-entry system. Figure 5.1 illustrates that the balance sheet shows where the capital of the business has come from and how this has been used in terms of providing assets, such as buildings, equipment, stocks of raw materials, balances in the bank, etc., after taking into account the liabilities, i.e. amounts owing to creditors for raw materials, shareholders for dividends, etc. Another way of looking at a balance sheet is shown in Figure 5.2.

In short, the balance sheet shows where all the finance comes from, for example ordinary share capital, loans, creditors, etc., and how this has been used, for instance how this finance is represented by the various assets. Note that the equation has changed to assets = capital + liabilities.

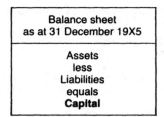

Figure 5.1 The balance sheet equation.

Capital and liabilities	Assets
Sources	**Uses**
Where finance came from	Where finance went to
What the business owes	What the business owns

Figure 5.2 What a balance sheet shows.

You should have noticed in Figure 5.1 that the balance sheet is prepared as at a specific date. This is frequently described **as a moment frozen in time**. It is not prepared to cover a period of time – it is, in fact, rather like a snapshot. A balance sheet prepared now may reveal a picture of health, but one prepared tomorrow, or in a week or a month's time, may reveal a completely different picture. Thus, the balance sheet has also been described as a position statement.

The figures reported in the balance sheet may have been affected by 'window dressing', i.e. manoeuvres which mean that the position which is being reported is either better (or worse) than it should be! For example, the stock level at the year end may have been run down, so that it is totally unrepresentative of the value of stock which was held throughout the year. The same goes for the debtors' and creditors' figures. This is important, because the balance sheet figures are used for interpretation and analytical purposes. For example, a lower stock figure will produce a higher rate of stock turnover figure; a lower debtors' figure will make the credit control ratios look better, and so on.

Although balance sheets can be adjusted for **inflation**, the majority of balance sheets which you are likely to encounter will have been prepared using 'historic cost' (i.e. the cost concept), for example certain assets are shown at their cost or cost less depreciation. Also, as mentioned in Chapter 2, the money measurement concept is applied to the construction of balance sheets. Only those items which can be measured in monetary terms are included. Thus, important factors such as good industrial relations, the quality of the management and morale cannot be shown in the balance sheet. This is illustrated in Figure 5.3.

SELF-ASSESSMENT

The balance sheet 1

From what we have looked at so far, plus a commonsense approach, see how you fare with the following self-assessment activity:

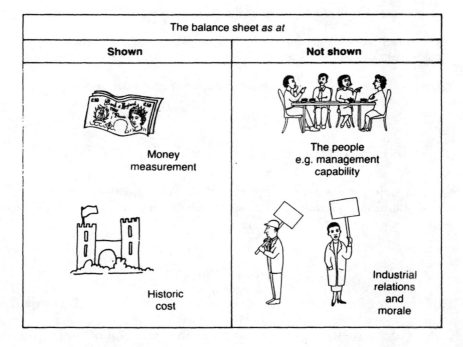

Figure 5.3 Balance sheet limitations.

1 Provide the missing words to complete the following sentences:

  (a) The balance sheet is not an account and not part of the double-entry system, it is simply a . . . of the financial position as at a certain date.

  (b) The balance sheet equation is capital = . . .

  (c) The capital and liabilities in a balance sheet show where the finance . . . and the assets show where the finance . . .

  (d) A balance sheet is prepared . . . a certain date. This is rather like a moment . . . in time.

2 List three factors which place limitations on the information provided in a balance sheet.

3 The value of the equipment shown in a balance sheet was arrived at, as follows:

Cost	Depreciation to date	Net (Book value)
£000	£000	£000
600	200	400

Explain briefly whether or not you consider that the company would be able to sell this equipment for £400,000.

4 Give one example of how window dressing can affect a balance sheet.

5 Which two concepts did we say particularly affect the figures which are reported in the balance sheet?

You will find the answers to these self-assessment problems on pages 175–176.

The internal balance sheet of a company

We will now have a look at the internal balance sheet of a company in pictorial format, Figure 5.4, to illustrate the layout and to help you understand the terminology.

Capital employed

This section of the balance sheet, as illustrated in Figure 5.4, shows the sources from which the capital invested in the business has been provided, such as share capital, reserves and long-term debt. All of these may be described as amounts owing because they are owing to whosoever provided them.

Share capital

This can be subdivided into two, as follows:

□ *Authorized share capital*
   This will only appear as a note on the balance sheet and refers to the maximum number of shares that can be issued by the company. The shares may be ordinary shares or preference shares – a contrast of their usual characteristics is shown in Figure 5.5. From Figure 5.5 it can be seen that the ordinary shareholders (frequently referred to as the equity shareholders) are the real entrepreneurs of a company, i.e. the real risk bearers.

□ *Issued share capital*
   The amounts shown represent the proportion of the nominal (or par, or face) value of shares (ordinary or preference), which have been received to date (see Figure 5.6). It can be observed from the three examples in Figure 5.6 that the nominal value per share is £1 and the amount which is received in excess of this value is called the share

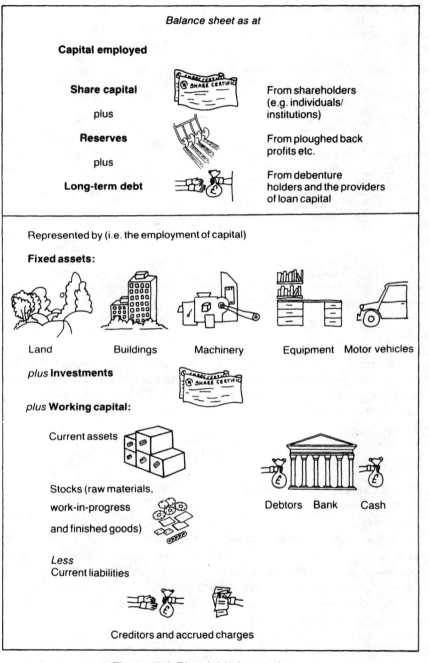

Figure 5.4 Pictorial balance sheet.

Characteristics	Ordinary shares	Preference shares
Voting rights	Yes, usually one vote per share	No, unless their dividends are in arrears
Dividends	Variable, according to the company's dividend policy	Usually a fixed percentage but some types may include participating rights
Winding up	Paid out last, i.e. they bear the greatest risk	Paid out before the ordinary shareholders
Repayable	Not usually except in the event of a winding up or special circumstances, e.g. redemption by the company of their own shares. This is why they are classed as permanent financing. However, they can be sold to third parties	They tend to be repayable between certain future dates
Rights	The rights of each class of share are laid down in the company's Memorandum and Articles of Association	

Figure 5.5 Characteristics of ordinary and preference shares.

premium. The balance, if any, which is to be paid at some future date for the shares is referred to as **calls**. Once shares have been issued and are fully paid and are then sold on the open market, the company does not receive any more money, apart from a very small transfer fee.

Reserves

Reserves can consist of the following:

□ *Share premium*
A kind of capital reserve representing the amount received from an issue of shares, over and above the nominal value of the shares. It may also be described as a statutory reserve, i.e. it can only be used for certain specific purposes laid down by company law, for example to provide the premium on the redemption of shares or debentures. It cannot be distributed as dividends.

□ *Capital reserves*
These may be caused by:
(a) the revaluation of fixed assets;

Example A: Issued 500,000 £1 ordinary shares for £1.50 per share (all monies received)	
Balance sheet (extract)	£000
Issued share capital	
500,000 £1 ordinary shares (fully paid)	500
Reserves	
Share premium (500,000 × 50p)	250

Example B: Issued 500,000 £1 ordinary shares at £1.50 but only £1.25 per share received to date	
Balance sheet (extract)	£000
Issued share capital	
500,000 £1 ordinary shares	500
Reserves	
Share premium (500,000 × 25p)	125

Example C: Issued 500,000 £1 ordinary shares at £1.50, but only 75p per share called up and received to date	
Balance sheet (extract)	£000
Issued share capital	
500.000 £1 ordinary shares (75p per share called up)	375

Figure 5.6 Shares and share premium.

(b) the acquisition of shares in a subsidiary company;
(c) the redemption of own shares.

□ *Revenue reserves*
These represent the profits which have been ploughed back into the company, i.e. retained profits or undistributed profits, and tend to comprise:
(a) general reserve – a reserve to which transfers are made from the profit and loss appropriation account;
(b) profit and loss account/retained earnings – the cumulative balance of the profit and loss appropriation account.

Many non-accountants have differing perceptions of what the balance sheet figure of reserves means. They tend to think of a reserve as being cash and/or bank balances which are kept on one side for emergencies. This is not so. The reason for this is that reserves are liabilities and not assets, i.e. amounts which have been invested in the business. The profits which have been retained and ploughed back into the business in most instances, belong to the ordinary shareholders. Thus, the stake of the ordinary shareholders in a company (sometimes called ordinary shareholders' interest or equity) is their ordinary share capital plus

Balance sheet (extract)	
Capital employed:	£000
Reserves	790
	———
Represented by:	
Assets	790
	———

Figure 5.7 What are reserves used for?

reserves. However, the reserves will be represented by a variety of assets, which could be cash, stock or fixed assets or investments (see Figure 5.7).

Long-term debt

Types of long-term debt include the following:

□ *Debentures*
A special type of loan, usually secured on an asset or assets belonging to the borrower. A debenture carries with it a legal obligation to pay interest by certain dates and to repay the capital.

□ *Long-term loans*
Obtained from banks and financial institutions.

□ *Bank overdraft*
This is a debatable item. Many companies nowadays use their overdraft (or a large proportion of it) as a long-term source of funds. However, its treatment could affect the ratios which are computed for analytical and comparative purposes.

Represented by

This major heading of the second section of the pictorial balance sheet in Figure 5.4 shows how the funds invested in the business have been deployed. Hence examples of other descriptions which are sometimes used include the employment of capital or uses.

Fixed assets

These are items which are bought for *use* in the business and not for resale, for example land, buildings, leasehold property, plant and machinery, office equipment, fixtures and fittings, motor vehicles, etc. Note that fixed assets (other than leasehold property) which are hired, leased or rented are not shown in the balance sheet because the company does not own them and has not bought them. However, details of such 'off-balance-sheet financing' will appear in a company's published accounts if it is a significant amount.

Investments

Investments refer to where a company has used its own funds to invest in stocks and shares.

Working capital

Working capital is sometimes called the circulating capital. It represents the difference between the current assets and the current liabilities. In effect it keeps the wheels of business turning by financing the everyday type of operating transactions.

Current assets

Current assets consist of the following:

☐ *Stocks*
These can be stocks of fuels, raw materials, work-in-progress and finished goods.

☐ *Debtors*
Debtors are customers who have not yet paid for goods supplied to them on credit. The figure in the balance sheet may, however, be reduced by the accumulated provision for bad and doubtful debts – an accounting process which is very similar to the way in which depreciation of fixed assets is dealt with.

☐ *Prepayments*
These can be goods or services already paid for, but which will not be used until the next (or a future) accounting period.

☐ *Bank balance.*

☐ *Cash balance.*

Current liabilities

Current liabilities are amounts owing which will tend to be settled within the next twelve months. Some examples of current liabilities are as follows:

☐ *Creditors*
The suppliers of goods to the business on credit which have not yet been paid for.

☐ *Accrued expenses*
The expenses for the current period which have not been paid.

☐ *Taxation*
The. amount owing for taxation.

☐ *Proposed dividend*
This is the amount owing to the shareholders for dividends.

☐ *Bank overdraft*
The bank overdraft can be considered as a current liability if it is not being used as a long-term source of funds.

You should note that the format of internal company balance sheets can and does vary. Examples of alternative formats are shown in Figures 5.8 and 5.9.

You may also have come across double-sided balance sheets. However, in an attempt to provide greater clarity the practice nowadays is to prepare vertical balance sheets; after all, the balance sheet is a statement and not an account!

For an alternative internal format for a balance sheet see Appendix 1 at the back of the book.

Intangible assets

In addition to the assets already mentioned there are also intangible assets. These are non-physical long-term assets such as the following:

☐ patents;
☐ copyrights;
☐ trade marks;
☐ brand names;

Balance sheet as at **Employment of capital** (i.e. represented by:)
Capital employed

Figure 5.8 An alternative format of the balance sheet.

Uses:	**Balance sheet as at** **Assets**
Sources:	**Capital** **and** **Liabilities**

Figure 5.9 Another alternative format of the balance sheet.

□ goodwill (see page 63);

□ certain research and development expenditure.

Before going any further see how you are getting on by attempting to answer the questions in the following self-assessment.

SELF-ASSESSMENT

The balance sheet 2

Please attempt the following 20 questions and then compare your answers with the suggested answers on pages 176–178.

1 Why is capital shown with the liabilities?

2 Which three groups of items, when taken together, can be described as capital employed?

3 Under which heading should debentures be shown?

4 How should the authorized share capital be shown?

5 Which class of shares normally has the voting rights?

6 Which class of shareholders has to bear the greatest risk?

7 Which class of shares receives a fixed dividend?

8 Give another name which is used to mean the nominal value of a share.

9 What is the amount called, which is received from an issue of shares over and above their nominal value?

10 What do revenue reserves represent?

11 Why are revenue reserves shown as liabilities?

12 What does the equity shareholders' interest in a company consist of?

13 Give two examples of items which are classed as long-term debt.

14 When should a bank overdraft not be shown as a current liability?

15 Why don't we show rented fixed assets in the balance sheet?

16 How is the working capital calculated?

17 In which section will the company's own proposed dividends be shown?

18 Where will a prepaid expense be shown?

19 In relation to ordinary shares, what are calls?

20 Give two causes of capital reserves.

How much is a business worth?

It has been said that a balance sheet will answer the question 'How much is the business worth?'. But does it? The balance sheet does provide *a* valuation – it tells us what the net worth (or net assets) amounts to. Figure 5.10 shows that the net worth can be calculated by either of the two methods illustrated.

However, we would only really know how much the business was

Method 1	Method 2
Total assets *less* **Current** **liabilities** e.g. Creditors, etc. = **Net assets** (net worth)	**Capital** *plus* **Reserves** *plus* **Long-term debt** = **Net assets** (net worth)

Figure 5.10 The calculation of net worth (net assets).

worth if it was sold. The assets would no doubt fetch a lot more or a lot less than their balance sheet values, i.e. book values. The amounts received would also depend upon whether or not the business was being sold as a going concern. If it was, an additional amount may be received for goodwill. **Goodwill** purchased represents the right to take over the orders, customers, organization and profit-earning capacity, etc. of the business which has been acquired. If the business was simply being liquidated, the assets would be sold at their break-up values, which are likely to be much lower than their going concern values.

EXAMPLE 5.1 Internal balance sheet

To conclude your study of this chapter we will now take a look at a more detailed balance sheet which has been prepared for internal reporting purposes as shown in Figure 5.11. As you work through this balance sheet, refer back to the appropriate reference in this chapter for any of the items which you are not clear about.

While studying the balance sheet in Figure 5.11 you should have noticed the following:

□ The company has not yet issued the whole of its ordinary share capital, i.e. £750,000 authorized and only £500,000 issued.

□ There are no calls, i.e. instalments due, on the ordinary or preference shares as indicated. The shares which have been issued are fully paid.

□ The company did issue the shares at a premium.

□ To date, the company has ploughed back into the business £60,000 by way of a general reserve and £75,000 retained earnings.

□ The rate of dividend on the preference shares and the rate of interest on the debentures reflect the going rate at the time of issue. Interest rates could be quite different today.

□ The freehold property is quite likely to be worth far more than its original cost, especially if it was acquired several years ago.

□ The investments could be subdivided into different classes, e.g. quoted and unquoted.

The balance sheet: The essence

The balance sheet is an accounting statement of assets, liabilities and capital prepared as at a specific date, i.e. a moment frozen in time. It is

Limited company balance sheet

Capital employed	£000	£000	£000
Authorized share capital			
£750,000 £1 ordinary shares		750	
£200,000 9% preference shares at £1 each		200	
		950	
Issued share capital			
£500,000 £1 ordinary shares (fully paid)		500	
£200,000 £1 9% preference shares (fully paid)		200	700
Reserves			
Share premium account		100	
General reserve		60	
Profit and loss account (retained earnings)		75	235
Capital plus reserves			935
Long-term debt			
100,000 £1 10% debentures		100	
Long-term loans		150	250
			£1,185

Employment of capital

Fixed assets	Cost	Depreciation to date	Net
	£000	£000	£000
Freehold property	600	—	600
Plant and machinery	240	140	100
Office equipment	110	50	60
Motor vehicles	100	60	40
	1,050	250	800

Investments			120
Working capital:			
Current assets			
Stock and work-in-progress	220		
Debtors less provision for bad debts	180		
Prepayments	30		
Bank	40		
Cash	10	480	
Less Current liabilities (falling due within one year)			
Creditors	110		
Accrued charges	30		
Taxation	25		
Proposed dividends	50	215	265
			£1,185

Figure 5.11 An internal balance sheet of a limited company.

A balance sheet	
Is:	**Is not:**
• a statement	• an account
• prepared as at a certain date	• drawn up to cover a period of time
• usually based on historic cost or historic cost less depreciation	• always a very good guide as to the value of the assets

Figure 5.12 What a balance sheet is and what a balance sheet is not.

not an account and not part of the double-entry bookkeeping/recording system. Figure 5.12 spells out what a balance sheet is and what it is not.

Other things to remember when dealing with the balance sheet are the balance sheet equation, which states that capital equals assets less liabilities, and also window dressing. Window dressing means making the balance sheet portray an untypical picture of the business, e.g. running down stocks or having a special effort on collecting money from debtors in the period leading up to the year end.

The language of the balance sheet

Capital employed
The capital employed consists of the following:

☐ *Issued share capital*
The amount invested in the company by the shareholders by way of ordinary shares/preference shares (see Figure 5.5).

☐ *Reserves*
There are several types of reserves, as follows:

(a) share premium – the amount which is received from an issue of shares over and above the nominal (par or face) value of the shares (see page 56);

(b) capital reserves – which may result from a revaluation of fixed assets; the acquisition of shares in a subsidiary company or the redemption of the company's own shares;

(c) revenue reserves – usually a general reserve and profit and loss account balance, both of which represent profits which have been ploughed back and retained in the business, i.e. the undistributed/retained earnings.

☐ *Long-term debt (or long-term liability)*
The following are examples of long-term debt:

   (a) debentures – a specialized type of loan usually secured by a charge on the assets of the company;
   (b) long-term loans – from banks/financial institutions.

The employment of capital
The employment of capital, i.e. the uses to which the capital employed has been applied, is made up of the following:

☐ *Fixed assets*
Assets owned by the company, which have been bought for use in the business and not for resale, e.g. land and buildings, machinery and plant, fixtures and fittings, office equipment, and motor vehicles.

☐ *Investments*
An example of investments is shares in other companies which have been purchased.

☐ *Working capital*
Current assets less current liabilities. This is the circulating capital of the business which is used to finance the everyday-type operating expenditure of the business.

☐ *Current assets*
These are made up of the following:

   (a) stocks of raw materials, fuels, work-in-progress and finished goods;
   (b) debtors, representing amounts owing from customers who have bought goods from the company on credit. To give a more realistic indication of this figure, the debtors may be reduced by a provision for bad and doubtful debts;
   (c) prepayments, deferred expenditure, i.e. paid out in the current accounting period but not yet consumed. The benefit of the expenditure extends beyond the current accounting period;
   (d) bank balance;
   (e) cash balance.

☐ *Current liabilities*
These are simply amounts due to be paid within the next twelve months which are owing to:

   (a) creditors and accrued expenses, for goods and services which have been supplied to the business/organization on credit.

(b) the tax authorities, for taxation.

(c) the shareholders, for proposed dividends which have not been paid.

For a more comprehensive picture see Figures 5.5 and 5.12.

Limitations

The usefulness of the balance sheet is limited because of the following:

☐ The time factor, i.e. the fact that it only shows the position at a particular moment in time, rather like a photograph.

☐ The application of the cost concept and the money measurement concept, i.e. items tend to be shown at their historic cost or historic cost less depreciation. Also items which cannot be measured in monetary terms cannot be shown, such as morale, good industrial relations, management expertise, etc.

☐ Valuation – the book value of the assets may be much less or much more than their real values. Thus, it is dangerous to say that a balance sheet will show us how much the assets are worth!

For an alternative balance sheet format please review the example on page 199.

Further reading

Bull, R. J., *Accounting in Business* (Butterworth, 1990).
Wood, F., *Business Accounting 1* (Pitman, 1993).

It is also recommended that you re-study Chapter 2, 'The concepts of financial accounting', to help consolidate your knowledge.

6

Depreciation of fixed assets

Objectives

The aim of this chapter is to show you how depreciation of fixed assets is calculated and how it is shown in the final accounts i.e. the trading and profit and loss account and the balance sheet.

When you have worked through this chapter, you should be able to do the following:

☐ Understand the reasons why depreciation has to be accounted for.

☐ Calculate the depreciation of fixed assets using:
  (a) the straight line method;
  (b) the reducing balance method;
  (c) the revaluation method.

☐ Appreciate how depreciation is shown in the trading and profit and loss account and the balance sheet.

☐ Follow the way in which disposals of fixed assets are dealt with.

Why charge depreciation?

The aim of depreciation is to spread the cost of the fixed asset over its useful life. To charge the full cost of a fixed asset as an expense in the profit and loss account of the year in which it was purchased, would simply not give a true and fair view of the profit or loss. It could in fact be described as a deferred expense; for instance, although the fixed asset is bought in one accounting period it is in effect consumed over a number of accounting periods.

The straight line method of depreciation

To calculate depreciation using the straight line method we need to know the following:

☐ The cost of the fixed asset.
☐ The life of the fixed asset.
☐ The residual value of the fixed asset at the end of its life (if any).

EXAMPLE 6.1 The straight line method of depreciation

A machine costs £6,000, has a life of four years and a residual value of £1,000 at the end of its life. The depreciation to be charged in the profit and loss account will be:

$$\frac{\text{Cost less residual value}}{\text{Life}} = \frac{£6,000 - £1,000}{4} = £1,250 \text{ per annum}$$

However, it is very difficult to estimate what the residual value is going to be in several years' time. The method may therefore ignore residual values which means that the calculation will be as illustrated in Example 6.2 which follows.

EXAMPLE 6.2 The straight line method of depreciation

The cost of some equipment will amount to £16,000 and its life is five years. The depreciation which would be charged to the profit and loss account would be:

$$\frac{\text{Cost}}{\text{Life}} = \frac{£16,000}{5} = £3,200 \text{ per annum}$$

This could also have been expressed in percentage terms, in this particular case at 20% on cost per year, i.e. 20% × £16,000 = £3,200 per annum.

SELF-ASSESSMENT

The straight line method of depreciation

Now see if you can compute the annual charge for depreciation for each of the fixed assets described below:

1 Fixtures and fittings costing £8,600, life ten years, residual value £400.

2 Office equipment costing £25,000, life eight years.

3 Plant and machinery costing £120,000, to be depreciated at 20% of cost per annum.

You will find the answers to these self-assessment questions on page 178.

The reducing balance method of depreciation

This method charges a percentage of cost in the first year and then a percentage of the book value (written down value or WDV) from the second year onwards. Thus, as the asset gets older the depreciation charge gets smaller.

EXAMPLE 6.3 The reducing balance method of depreciation

An estate car costing £12,000 is to be written off at 25% reducing balance per year. The depreciation figures for the first three years would be:

	Cost or WDV	Depreciation at 25%	WDV (i.e. book value)
	£000	£000	£000
Estate car			
Year 1	12	3	9
Year 2	9	2.25	6.75
Year 3	6.75	1.6875	5.0625

and so on, rounding the numbers as you think fit.

SELF-ASSESSMENT

The reducing balance method of depreciation

By following the workings shown in Example 6.3, work out the depreciation charge for each of the three years for a car costing £8,000 to be depreciated at 25% reducing balance per year.

You will find the answers to this self-assessment exercise on page 178.

The revaluation method of depreciation

For certain fixed assets, for example contractor's plant and equipment, tools, cutlery and crockery, the revaluation method may be considered more appropriate. The reason for this is the uncertain condition of the asset at the end of the accounting period.

EXAMPLE 6.4 The revaluation method of depreciation

The depreciation under the revaluation method is simply the difference between the opening value of the asset at the start of the accounting period and the closing value of the asset at the end of the accounting period.

An hotel had a stock of crockery and cutlery at the start of the year of £3,400. At the end of the year it was valued at £2,950. The depreciation, therefore, will be £3,400 less £2,950, which equals £450.

SELF-ASSESSMENT

The revaluation method of depreciation

Details relating to some contractor's plant were as follows:

Plant	Start of year	End of year
	£000	£000
Year 1 valuations	56	49
Year 2 valuations	49	33

You are required to calculate the depreciation for years 1 and 2.

You will find the answers to this self-assessment exercise on page 178.

Accounting for depreciation

Depreciation is the charge made in the profit and loss account for the use and wear and tear of fixed assets. It does not provide funds for the replacement of fixed assets. Funds can only be provided for the replacement of fixed assets if cash is put on one side for that purpose, for instance paid into a special account which is to be used to replace fixed assets.

There are two systems for dealing with the depreciation charge, as follows:

□ *System 1*
In the year of purchase charge a full year's depreciation irrespective of the date on which the fixed asset was acquired, and in the year of sale charge no depreciation at all.

□ *System 2*
The time apportionment system charges depreciation on a time basis from the date it is purchased right up to the date on which the fixed asset is disposed of.

If you have an examination problem which does not specify which system is being used you are advised to opt for system 1 which is easier to operate.

The ledger accounts and final accounts

The fixed asset account records the cost of the fixed asset. The provision for depreciation account stores the cumulative depreciation figure, i.e. the depreciation to date. The difference between the two accounts is the book value, i.e. written down value, the figure which in a balance sheet may simply be called the net.

The annual amount of depreciation will be charged as an expense in the profit and loss account and added to the cumulative depreciation to date brought forward from last year in the provision for depreciation account. This figure, i.e. last year's depreciation to date brought forward plus this year's profit and loss charge, is the figure which will be deducted from the cost of the fixed asset in the balance sheet, in order to arrive at the net (net book value).

The profit or loss on the sale of a fixed asset

The profit or loss on the sale of a fixed asset is found by the following equation:

Sale proceeds of fixed asset less book value = profit or loss on sale

Note the treatment of depreciation of fixed assets and the sale of fixed assets in Chapter 8, in connection with funds flow/cash flow statements.

Depreciation of fixed assets: The essence

Depreciation is treated as an expense in the profit and loss account in an attempt to spread the cost of the fixed asset over its useful life. The charge is there to cover the use and wear and tear of the fixed asset. However, please note that charging depreciation does not provide for the replacement of fixed assets. Only if cash is put away can we provide the cash needed to replace fixed assets.

There are a number of different methods which can be used for charging depreciation in the profit and loss account. Three of the methods being the following:

☐ The straight line method.
☐ The reducing balance method.
☐ The revaluation method.

The depreciation can be charged to the profit and loss account using one of the following systems:

☐ *System 1*
Charge a full year's depreciation in the year of purchase and none in the year of sale.

☐ *System 2*
Time apportionment – depreciate the fixed asset from the date of purchase right up to the date of sale.

Accounting for depreciation

The fixed asset account will be kept at cost. The provision for depreciation account records the cumulative depreciation to date and the difference between these two accounts equals the book value (or WDV, or net). The amount charged in the profit and loss account will also be added to the provision for depreciation account.

The balance sheet entry will be the cost of the fixed asset, less depreciation to date which equals the net (book value). See the balance sheet of a limited company in Chapter 5 (Figure 5.11) on page 64 for specimen calculations for the fixed assets.

Further reading

Langley, F. P. and Hardern, G. S., *Introduction to Accounting for Business Studies* (Butterworth, 1994).
Wood, F., *Business Accounting 1* (Pitman, 1993).

7

Preparing a trading and profit and loss account and a balance sheet from a trial balance

Objectives

It is not the aim of this chapter that you become an expert in this mechanical process. The idea of giving you the experience of preparing final accounts (i.e. trading and profit and loss account and balance sheet) from a trial balance plus further information, is to:

☐ Enable you to appreciate some of the problems involved with income measurement, i.e. the way in which we work out the profit or loss for a period.

☐ Help you to understand more fully the terminology which is used.

☐ Know how the value of certain assets, such as plant and machinery, motor vehicles and debtors, has been arrived at.

☐ Give you a deeper understanding of the figures which are used.

When you reach the end of this chapter you should be able to do the following:

☐ Sort out the debit and credit items listed in the trial balance into fixed assets, current assets, investments, expenses of the profit and loss account, sales and cost of sales data for the trading account, issued share capital, reserves, long-term debt and current liabilities.

☐ Adopt and use a systematic approach to prepare the trading and profit and loss account (including an appropriation account) and balance sheet of a limited company from a trial balance plus adjustments, for internal reporting purposes.

The preparation of a trading and profit and loss account and a balance sheet from a trial balance, plus adjustments for internal reporting purposes

We will work through a step-by-step example. You are provided with the following information relating to Scholes Manufacturing Ltd.

Trial balance at 31 December 19X2

Destination	(1) Liabilities, income and capital:	Debit £000	Credit £000	(2) + or − Adjustment £000	(3) Balance sheet effect £000
	Sales		180		
	£1 ordinary shares		100		
	Creditors		17		
	Long-term loan		50		
	Bank overdraft		13		
	Balance on profit and loss account 31 December 19X1		46		
	Accumulated depreciation to 31 December 19X1 on fixtures and fittings		20		
	Accumulated depreciation on motor vans to 31 December 19X1		18		
	Assets and expenses:				
	Trade debtors	40			
	Purchases	87			
	Opening stock 1 January 19X2	23			
	Property at cost	120			
	Fixtures and fittings (cost)	50			
	Motor vans (cost)	36			
	Directors' salaries	34			
	Wages	27			
	Office expenditure	7			
	Selling expenses	19			
	Bank interest and charges	1			
		444	444		

Note the following adjustments:

1. Stock on hand at 31 December 19X2 is valued at cost, £21,000.
2. Depreciation on fixtures and fittings is calculated at 10% of cost per annum.
3. Accrued office expenditures (heat and light, telephone) are estimated at £2,000.
4. Selling expenses include prepaid advertising for 19X3 of £4,000.
5. Depreciation on motor vehicles is calculated at 25% of cost, per annum.

Step 1: Knowing the destination of an item

Remembering Figure 3.10, 'The trial balance and ALICE', we can infer the following:

A *Assets* will be shown in the balance sheet.

L *Liabilities* will also be shown in the balance sheet.

I *Income* will be shown in the trading account (income from trading) and the profit and loss account (non-trading income, e.g. rent received).

C *Capital* (and reserves) will be shown in the balance sheet.

E *Expenses* will be shown in the trading account if they are part of the cost of sales, and the profit and loss account if they are not.

Debit balances: **Credit balances:**

Assets

                  Liabilities
                  Income
                  Capital and reserves

Expenses

However, movements in the profit and loss account (retained profits/retained earnings) and general reserve, dividends paid and payable for the year, and taxation will be dealt with in the profit and loss appropriation account (see also Figures 4.4 and 4.7).

Thus, step 1 involves marking each item listed in the trial balance in the destination column (1) as follows:

B/C   = Balance sheet / Capital

B/Res   = Balance sheet / Reserves

B/FA   = Balance sheet / Fixed asset

B/CA   = Balance sheet / Current asset

B/I   = Balance sheet / Investment

B/CL   = Balance sheet / Current liability
B/LTD = Balance sheet / Long-term debt
T   = Trading account
P&L   = Profit and loss account
App   = Profit and loss appropriation account

This simple procedure highlights the statement/account to which an item belongs and the (group) section to which it belongs. The following example of a trial balance is the same as the one which appeared on page 76, but with the 'destination' column completed.

Trial balance at 31 December 19X2

(1)					(2)	(3)
Destination	Liabilities, income and capital:	Debit £000	Credit £000		+ or − Adjustment £000	Balance sheet effect £000
T	Sales		180			
B/C	£1 ordinary shares		100			
B/CL	Creditors		17			
B/LTD	Long-term loan		50			
B/CL	Bank overdraft		13			
App	Balance on profit and loss account 31 December 19X1		46			
−B/FA	Accumulated depreciation to 31 December 19X1 on fixtures and fittings		20			
−B/FA	Accumulated depreciation to 31 December 19X1 on motor vans		18			
	Assets and expenses:					
B/CA	Trade debtors	40				
T	Purchases	87				
T	Opening stock 1 January 19X2	23				
B/FA	Property at cost	120				
B/FA	Fixtures and fittings (cost)	50				
B/FA	Motor vans (cost)	36				
P&L	Directors' salaries	34				
P&L	Wages	27				
P&L	Office expenditure	7				
P&L	Selling expenses	19				
P&L	Bank interest and charges	1				
		444	444			

Note that the opening stock at 1 January 19X2 goes to the trading account. It is the closing stock which is adjusted after the trial balance, which will appear in the balance sheet. This is because it is the stock as at the balance sheet date, i.e. 31 December 19X2 in this particular case. The opening stock, shown as an asset in last year's balance sheet, in effect, becomes an expense of the current period, any which remains being included in the closing stock.

Step 2: Dealing with the adjustments

You must remember that the adjustments will have a dual effect. They will affect the trading account or profit and loss account or the profit and loss appropriation account and the balance sheet.

For example, accruals and prepayments are taken into account in the profit and loss account so that the correct expense for the period is charged in computing the profit or loss for that period. The accruals and prepayments also appear in the balance sheet as follows:

□ Accruals to indicate that the expenditure is still owing at the balance sheet date are shown as a current liability.
□ Prepayments to represent expenditure already paid out, but which belongs to the next (or future) accounting periods are shown as a current asset.

The adjustments can be marked as to their destinations, as follows (where: T = trading account; P&L = profit and loss account; and B = balance sheet):

T or P&L	B	Note	Adjustments
T	CA	1.	Stock on hand at 31 December 19X2 is valued at cost, £21,000.
P&L	−FA	2.	Depreciation on fixtures and fittings is calculated at 10% of cost per annum
P&L	CL	3.	Accrued office expenditure (heat and light, telephone) is estimated at £2,000.
P&L	CA	4.	Selling expenses include prepaid advertising for 19X3 of £4,000.
P&L	−FA	5.	Depreciation on motor vehicles is calculated at 25% of cost per annum.

Having marked the dual effect regarding the adjustments, as a means to promote greater accuracy the effects of the adjustments are shown in columns (2) and (3) of the trial balance sheet as follows:

Trial balance at 31 December 19X2

(1)		(2)			(3)
Destination	Liabilities, income and capital:	Debit £000	Credit £000	+ or − Adjustment £000	Balance sheet effect £000
T	Sales		180		
B/C	£1 ordinary shares		100		
B/CL	Creditors		17		
B/LTD	Long-term loan		50		
B/CL	Bank overdraft		13		
App	Balance on profit and loss account 31 December 19X1		46		(See appropriation account)
−B/FA	Accumulated depreciation to 31 December 19X1 on fixtures and fittings		20	Depreciation +5 P&L	FA − 25 to date
−B/FA	Accumulated depreciation on motor vans to 31 December 19X1		18	Depreciation +9 P&L	FA − 27 to date
	Assets and expenses:				
B/CA	Trade debtors	40		Closing	
T	Purchases	87		stock	
T	Opening stock 1 January 19X2	23		−21 T	21 (CA)
B/FA	Property at cost	120			
B/FA	Fixtures and fittings (cost)	50			
B/FA	Motor vans (cost)	36			
P&L	Directors' salaries	34			
P&L	Wages	27			
P&L	Office expenditure	7		+2 Accrual	2 (CL)
P&L	Selling expenses	19		−4 Prepaid	4 (CA)
P&L	Bank interest and charges	1			
		444	444		

Thus the effect of each adjustment on the trading and profit and loss account and the balance sheet has been recorded and highlighted in columns (2) and (3) and illustrates the dual effect.

Step 3: Prepare the trading and profit and loss account

This task is a matter of scanning the above data and picking up the trading account information first, and computing the gross profit, and then picking up the profit and loss information and computing the net profit (or loss).

As you transfer each item from the trial balance to the trading and profit and loss account, it is a good idea to tick it off. This should help to ensure that all the items are dealt with. Thus the trading and profit and loss account for the year ended 31 December 19X2 for Scholes Manufacturing Ltd will appear as follows:

Scholes Manufacturing Ltd
Trading and profit and loss account for the year ended 31 December 19X2

	£000	£000	£000
Sales			180
Less **Cost of sales:**			
Opening stock (at 1 January 19X2)		23	
Add Purchases		87	
		110	
Less Closing stock (at 31 December 19X2)		21	89
Gross profit			91
Less **Expenses:**			
Directors' salaries		34	
Wages		27	
Office expenditure	7		
Add Accrual	2	9	
Selling expenses	19		
Less Prepayment	4	15	
Bank interest and charges		1	
Depreciation:			
Fixtures and fittings	5		
Motor vans	9	14	100
Net loss before tax			(£9)
P&L account b/f			46
Balance c/f			£37

The £37,000 P&L account balance at 31 December 19X2 is the figure which will go in this year's balance sheet, reserves section.

Step 4: Prepare the balance sheet

All the unticked items in the trial balance should be balance sheet items. They should be picked up in the order in which they are required, as dictated by the format which is used and adjusted to take account of the further information which is contained in the notes. As you transfer an item from the trial balance to the balance sheet, tick it off. Thus the balance sheet as at 31 December 19X2 for Scholes Manufacturing Ltd will appear as follows:

Scholes Manufacturing Ltd
Balance sheet as at 31 December 19X2

Capital employed

Authorized share capital	not given		
	£000	£000	£000
Issued share capital			
Ordinary shares of £1			100
Reserves			
Retained earnings (P&L account)			37
			137
Long-term debt			
Debentures		Nil	
Loans		50	50
			£187

Employment of capital

	Cost	Depreciation to date	Net
	£000	£000	£000
Fixed assets			
Property	120	Nil	120
Fixtures and fittings	50	25	25
Motor vans	36	27	9
	206	52	154
Working capital:			
Current assets			
Stock		21	
Debtors		40	
Prepayments		4	
Bank (overdraft)		(13)	
		52	
Less			
Current liabilities			
Creditors	17		
Accruals	2	19	33
			£187

SELF-ASSESSMENT

Port Peter plc

The trial balance of Port Peter plc extracted from the accounting records at 31 December 19X4 is as follows:

(1)		(2)	(3)
Destination (Jumbled up) details	Debit Credit	+ or − Adjustment	Balance sheet effect
	£000 £000	£000	£000
Authorized and issued £1 ordinary shares	400		
Sales	375		
Purchases	140		
Stock 1 January 19X4	29		
Share premium	25		
Bad debts (written off)	3		
Wages and salaries	48		
Motor vehicles (at cost)	40		
Depreciation to date on motor vehicles	16		
Motor expenses	9		
Overhead expenses*	30		
Freehold land and buildings	437		
Debtors	28		
Creditors	23		
Bank balance	32		
Profit and loss account	11		
10% debentures	50		
Directors' fees	56		
Taxation	— —		
Fixtures, fittings and equipment (at cost)	80		
Depreciation to date on fixtures and fittings and equipment	30		
Provision for bad debts	2		
	£932 £932		

*Includes debenture interest of £5,000.

The following data are also available:

Note

1. Depreciation of fixed assets is to be provided as follows:
   (a) fixtures, fittings and equipment at 10% of cost per annum;
   (b) motor vehicles at 20% of cost per annum.

2. Rent prepaid included in the overhead expenses amounted to £4,000.

3. The directors propose to pay a dividend for the year of £30,000 to the ordinary shareholders.

4. The stock at 31 December 19X4 amounted to £20,000.

5. The estimated corporation tax for the year is £18,000.

See if you can complete the destination column (1), the adjustments column (2) and the balance sheet effect column (3) and then compare your attempt with the solution which appears on page 179.

Having compared your answers with the solution given on page 179, we can prepare the trading and profit and loss account and the balance sheet for Port Peter plc as follows:

Port Peter plc
Trading and profit and loss account for the year ended 31 December 19X4

	£000	£000	£000
Sales			375
Less **Cost of sales:**			
Opening stock		29	
Add Purchases		140	
		169	
Less Closing stock		20	149
Gross profit			226
Less **Expenses:**			
Bad debts		3	
Wages and salaries		48	
Motor expenses		9	
Overhead expenses	30		
Less Rent prepaid	4	26	
Directors' fees		56	
Depreciation:			
Fixtures, fittings and equipment	8		
Motor vehicles	8	16	158
Net profit before tax			68
Appropriations:			
Corporation tax			18
Net profit after tax			50
Proposed dividend			30
			20
Add Balance b/f from last year			11
P&L account balance c/f			£31

Port Peter plc
Balance sheet as at 31 December 19X4

Capital employed

	£000
Authorized share capital	400
400,000 £1 ordinary shares	

	£000	£000	£000
Issued share capital			
Ordinary shares			400
Reserves			
Share premium		25	
Retained earnings (P&L account balance)		31	56
			456
Long-term debt			
Debentures			50
			£506

Employment of capital

	Cost	Depreciation to date	Net
	£000	£000	£000
Fixed assets			
Freehold land and buildings	437	Nil	437
Fixtures, fittings and equipment	80	38	42
Motor vehicles	40	24	16
	557	62	495
Working capital:			
Current assets			
Stock		20	
Debtors	28		
Less provision for bad debts	2	26	
Prepayments	—	4	
Bank		32	
		82	
Less			
Current liabilities			
Creditors	23		
Taxation	18		
Proposed dividend	30	71	11
	—	—	506

SELF-ASSESSMENT

Chua Lim Ltd

From the following information provided see if you can prepare a trading and profit and loss account for the year to 30 June 19X5 and a balance sheet as at that date. When you have completed your attempt, compare your answer with the suggested answer which is provided on pages 180–2.

Trial balance 30 June 19X5	Debit £000	Credit £000
Ordinary shares authorized and issued, fully paid in £1 shares		800
Share premium account		80
10% debentures		100
Profit and loss account balance		30
Freehold land and buildings at cost	850	
Plant and machinery at cost	160	
Vehicles at cost	40	
Provision for depreciation on plant and machinery		36
Provision for depreciation of vehicles		16
Sales and purchases	700	998
Stock at 1 July 19X4	94	
Debtors and creditors	85	98
General expenses	15	
Salaries	104	
Discount allowed and received	2	6
Directors' fees	72	
Provision for bad and doubtful debts		3
Debenture interest	10	
Telephone, stationery and printing	2	
Rates and insurance	5	
Audit fees	1	
Interim dividend paid to ordinary shareholders	16	
Cash and bank balances	11	
	£2,167	£2,167

The following information is also available:

Note

1. The closing stock at 30 June 19X5 amounted to £106,000.

2. The rates and insurance figure includes £1,000 paid in advance.

3. Depreciation on plant and machinery is at 10% of cost per annum.

4. Depreciation of motor vehicles is at 25% of book value (i.e. 25% of cost less depreciation).

5. The provision for bad debts is to be increased by £4,000.

6. Corporation tax for the year is estimated at £25,000.

7. The proposed final dividend for the year is £20,000.

For an alternative internal format for the final accounts, see Appendix 1, pages 198 and 199.

Preparing final accounts from a trial balance: The essence

A systematic approach needs to be adopted. One suggested approach is as follows:

☐ *Step 1*

Mark each item which appears in the trial balance with its destination/location in the final accounts, for example the following:

(a) B/CA = Balance sheet item current asset;

(b) T   = Trading account item;

(c) P&L = Profit and loss account item;

(d) App = Appropriation account item; and so on.

☐ *Step 2*

Take into account the dual effect of adjustments and mark them either in the notes/adjustments section of the information supplied and/or combine it with the item to which it relates in the trial balance and note its effect on the balance sheet.

☐ *Step 3*

Know well the format which you intend to use for the trading and profit and loss account. Scan the trial balance to pick up the information as you need it. Having transferred it to the trading and profit and loss account, tick it off in the trial balance to signify that it has been dealt with.

☐ *Step 4*

Know well your balance sheet layout. Pick up the items from the trial balance as you need them and, having transferred them to the balance sheet, tick off each item concerned.

Finally, remember Figure 3.10 – The trial balance and ALICE. This is a great help during the sorting process, because debit items are either assets, investments or expenses.

Further reading

Pizzey, A., *Accounting and Finance: A Firm Foundation* (Cassell, 1994).
Wood, F., *Business Accounting 1* (Pitman, 1993).

8

Funds flow and cash flow statements

Objectives

The principal objectives of this chapter are that by the time you have worked carefully through it, you should be able to do the following:

☐ Appreciate why a funds flow is necessary in order to explain what has happened to the following:
   (a) cash;
   (b) profits;
   (c) working capital.

☐ Understand the flow of business funds as illustrated in Figure 8.1.

☐ Prepare a funds flow statement explaining what has happened to cash and bank balances from a comparison of balance sheets, including an *FRS 1* cash flow statement.

☐ Prepare a funds flow to explain what has happened to working capital.

☐ Deal with problems involving the sale of a fixed asset.

Why a funds flow?

The profit and loss account of a business shows how much profit or loss was earned during an accounting period and how it has been arrived at. However, it does not show what has happened to it. The balance sheet shows the resources of the business at the beginning and end of the accounting period, but it cannot clearly show the movements in capital, reserves, long-term debt, assets and liabilities.

In order to answer the questions 'what has happened to cash, or profits?' and 'what has happened to working capital?' we need to draw up a statement of sources and applications of funds, or funds flow for short.

The objectives of the funds flow are to show the following over an accounting period:

☐ The way in which the business has financed its operations.

☐ The sources from which funds have been derived, for example share capital, loans, profits, etc.

☐ The way in which the funds have been used, for instance to buy stocks of raw materials or fixed assets.

In short, funds flow shows how a business has financed its assets, for example from long-term sources or out of working capital.

In addition to a profit and loss account and the balance sheet, the published accounts of UK companies also include a cash flow statement. However, the information which is used to produce it is in fact a selection or a reclassification and summary of the information contained in the profit and loss account and the balance sheet.

The flow of business funds

A study of Figure 8.1 shows that money can come into a business from a number of sources. It can come in from:

☐ Shareholders.

☐ Loans.

☐ Sale of fixed assets.

☐ Cash sales.

☐ Cash from debtors, etc.

This money can be used to pay:

☐ Dividends to shareholders.

☐ Interest on loans and also to repay the loans.

☐ Creditors and expenses.

☐ For materials.

☐ For fixed assets.

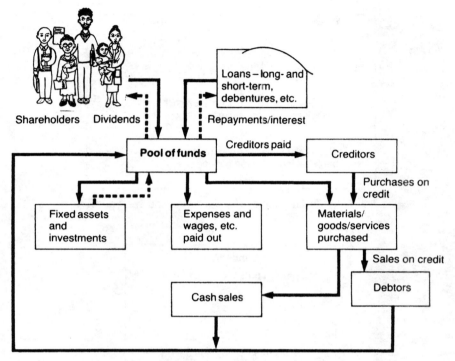

Figure 8.1 The flow of business funds.

The longer-term funds from share capital and loans tend to be used to finance the purchase of fixed assets and provide a certain portion of the working capital.

The working capital shown in Figure 8.1, i.e. the current assets and current liabilities, tends to be used to finance the everyday-type operating expenses, such as wages and various overheads. Thus, you can see why it is also called the circulating capital. As transactions take place its form changes, for example if materials are bought on credit, stock goes up and creditors go up.

What has happened to cash?

A statement of source and application of funds can be drafted to answer the above question. The logic behind the calculation is quite easy to follow and understand, as illustrated by Figure 8.2. An alternative way of showing the same information is given in Figure 8.3.

In effect, Figure 8.3 is saying that what we start off with plus what we receive in the period should equal what we spend plus what we have left.

Funds flow

Sources of funds coming into the business during the period under review

less

Applications, i.e. the uses to which those funds were applied during that period

equals

The increase or decrease in the cash and bank balances for the period

Figure 8.2 A funds flow for explaining what has happened to cash.

Funds flow

Opening balance of cash/bank

plus

Sources

equals

Applications plus (or minus) the closing balance of cash/bank

Figure 8.3 An alternative funds flow for explaining what has happened to cash.

If we spend more than we have, we end up with a negative amount, i.e. an overdraft.

Comparing balance sheets

It is possible to produce a funds flow by simply comparing the current year's figures in the balance sheet with last year's figures.

We will use the following example of Dom Dank U plc, to show you how this somewhat oversimplified type of funds flow is prepared. Then, having dealt with the mechanics, we will take an in-depth view of the figures to answer the following questions:

□ Why is a particular item shown as a source?
□ Why is a particular item shown as an application?

EXAMPLE 8.1 Dom Dank U plc

Dom Dank U plc

Balance sheet data

19X6		19X7
£000	**Capital employed**	£000
800	Issued share capital	1,200
500	Profit and loss account	800
600	Long-term loans	340
1,900		2,340

Employment of capital
Fixed assets

Cost	Depreciation to date	Net		Cost	Depreciation to date	Net
£000	£000	£000		£000	£000	£000
800	—	800	Buildings	1,340	—	1,340
900	200	700	Plant and machinery	1,000	250	750
100	40	60	Motor vehicles	120	50	70
1,800	240	1,560		2,460	300	2,160

Working capital
Current assets

19X6		19X7
180	Stock	260
120	Debtors	100
200	Bank	120
500		480
	Current liabilities	
160	Creditors	300
340		180
1,900		2,340

Statement of source and application of funds (funds flow)

		Workings			
		19X6	19X7		
Sources		£000	£000		£000
	Issued share capital	(800 to 1200)			400
	Profit and loss account				
	(i.e. retained earnings)	(500 to 800)			300
	Depreciation plant and machinery	(200 to 250)			50
	Depreciation motor vehicles	(40 to 50)			10
	Debtors	(120 to 100)			20
	Creditors	(160 to 300)			140
					920
Less	**Applications**			£000	
	Long-term loans	(600 to 340)		260	
	Buildings	(800 to 1340)		540	
	Plant and machinery (cost)	(900 to 1000)		100	
	Motor vehicles (cost)	(100 to 120)		20	
	Stock	(180 to 260)		80	1,000
	Decrease in bank balance	(200 to 120)			(80)

An alternative format using the same information could be:

		£000	£000
	Opening bank balance (19X6)	200	
Add	Sources (as above)	920	1,120
Less	Applications (as above)		1,000
Equals	Closing bank balance (19X7)		£120

Both of these help to answer the question 'what has happened to cash?'

Having completed the statement of source and application of funds for
Dom Dank U plc we can now reflect on the treatment of each item.
    Why are the following shown as sources?

☐ *Issued share capital*
    This is the result of more money coming in from shareholders for shares
    which have been issued to them.

☐ *Profit and loss account*
    The increase represents the profits for the current accounting period
    which have been ploughed back and retained in the business.

□ *Depreciation*
Because depreciation is a non-cash item, and because it was deducted in computing profits it has to be added back as a source. You are, in effect, adding it back on to the profits (or loss) to get them back to what they were before the depreciation for the period under review was deducted.

□ *Debtors*
The decrease in debtors means that the debtors in question have paid, or another way of looking at it is that Dom Dank U plc are giving less in total credit to their customers. This could be due to them collecting their outstanding debts more quickly.

□ *Creditors*
This is a source because the creditors are in fact providing the company with more short-term finance. This may be the result of an increase in the level of activity and/or a slowing down in the time taken to pay the creditors.

Why are the following shown as applications?

□ *Long-term loans*
The reduction indicates that a lump sum (in this case £260,000) has been paid off the long-term loans. This could be one of the reasons why they received more share capital.

□ *Fixed assets (buildings, plant and machinery, and motor vehicles)*
These were arrived at by comparing the cost figures only and represent the amounts spent acquiring new fixed assets during the current year (i.e. 19X7).

□ *Stock*
This is an application because more money is being tied up in stock.

The sources comprise all of the new finance which came in during the year, i.e. 19X7. Assets, such as buildings, stock, etc. represent capital tied up, therefore, if they increase more finance is being used and tied up in those assets.

SELF-ASSESSMENT

Iainwar Ltd

Now, it is your turn. See if you can produce a funds flow from the information which is provided in the following balance sheet for Iainwar Ltd.

Iainwar Ltd

		19X7 £000		19X6 £000
Sources of capital				
Share of capital		60		50
Profit and loss account		96		80
		—		—
Shareholders' funds		156		130
Long-term loans		70		40
		—		—
		226		170
		—		—
Employment of capital				
Fixed assets:				
Freehold property		135		105
Plant and equipment				
Cost	72		54	
Depreciation	38	34	28	26
	—		—	
Motor vehicles				
Cost	32		20	
Depreciation	19	13	10	10
	—	—	—	—
		182		141
Current assets:				
Stock	64		27	
Debtors	51		22	
Cash at bank	—		10	
	—		—	
	(A) 115		59	
	—		—	
Less **Current liabilities:**				
Creditors	39		30	
Bank overdraft	32		—	
	—		—	
	(B) 71		30	
	—			
Net current assets: (A) − (B)		44		29
		—		—
		226		170
		—		—

When you have completed your answer, compare it with the suggested answer provided on page 183.

The cash flow statement (FRS 1)

The cash flow statement should help you understand the reasons for the movement of cash during an accounting period. The formats adopted for reporting purposes (i.e. the published accounts), in the United Kingdom are prescribed by FRS 1 (Financial Reporting Standard) and cover the following major headings:

☐ net cash in/outflow from operating activities;
☐ returns on investments and the servicing of finance;
☐ taxation;
☐ investing activities;
☐ financing.

The final figure is the *increase/decrease in cash and cash equivalent*, e.g. an increase or decrease in the bank balance (Figure 8.4).

The net cash flow from operating activities may have to be computed by taking into account the increase/decrease in retained earnings, depreciation

---

Cash flow statement for year ended 31 December 19x7

	£	£
Net cash flow from operating activities		
Returns on investments, and the servicing of finance		
Dividends received		
Dividends paid		
Interest paid		
	___	___
Taxation		
Tax paid		
		___
Investing activities		
Purchase of tangible fixed assets		
Sale of tangible fixed assets		
Proceeds from sale of trade investments		
	___	___
Financing		
Proceeds from new share capital		
Repayment of borrowings		
	___	___
Increase (or decrease) in cash and cash equivalents		___

Figure 8.4 An *FRS 1* cash flow statement.

EXAMPLE 8.2   Cash flow statement for Jean Ltd

Jean Ltd
Balance sheet as at 31 December 19X8

Capital employed	This year 19X8			Last year 19X7		
	£000	£000	£000	£000	£000	£000
Authorized share capital –						
ordinary shares			600			600
			—			—
Issued share capital						
Ordinary shares of £1 each			450			300
Reserves						
Undistributed profits						
(i.e. P&L balance)			30			14
			—			—
Capital plus reserves			480			314
Long-term debts						
11% debentures			50			120
			—			—
			£530			£434
			—			—

Represented by		Depreciation			Depreciation	
Fixed assets	Cost	to date	Net	Cost	to date	Net
	£000	£000	£000	£000	£000	£
Land and buildings	320	Nil	320	280	Nil	280
Plant and machinery	152	50	102	130	24	106
	—	—	—	—	—	—
	472	50	422	410	24	386
	—	—		—	—	
Working capital						
Current assets						
Stock	90			50		
Debtors	50			35		
Cash at bank	20	160		14	99	
	—			—		
Less **Current liabilities**						
Creditors	30			36		
Proposed dividend	10			7		
Taxation	12	52	108	8	51	48
	—	—	—	—	—	—
			530			£434
			—			—

Profit and loss appropriation account (extract) for the year ended 31 December 19X8 (this year)

	£000s
Net profit before taxation*	38
Less Corporation tax based on this year's profits	12
	26
Less Proposed dividend	10
Undistributed profit for this year	16
Add Balance brought forward (from last year)	14
	30

*After depreciation £26,000 and interest on debentures £9,000.

charged for the period, and profits/losses on the sale of fixed assets, interest paid, tax appropriated, dividends appropriated and movements in stocks, debtors and creditors.

A much quicker way of computing it, provided the information is available is to take the net profit before interest and tax (NPBIT) and add back depreciation and losses on sales of fixed assets (less any profits on the sale of fixed assets) and then adjust for the movements in stocks, debtors and creditors.

From your observations of Figure 8.4 of the statement, you should be able to see how much cash went out during the period on dividends, taxation, new fixed assets and the repayment of borrowings and how these were financed, e.g. from ploughed back profits, the sale of fixed assets and new borrowings.

You should be able to see how cash is moving through the organization and the net impact on the cash balance at the year end. It informs the user where the cash came from and where it went to. It should help investors, creditors, and other users to determine the relationship between income and cash flows and provide an indication of the availability of each for dividends and long-term investment; it should also help users and managers to demonstrate the firm's ability to finance growth from internal sources.

We will now, using the information provided in Example 8.2 Jean Ltd, prepare a cash flow statement in the *FRS 1* format, via a step by step illustration with a commentary.

☐ *Step 1*

Compute the net cash flow from operating activities, as follows:

	£000
Retained profits (*this is taken from the profit and loss account* but could be calculated from the Balance Sheet, i.e. 30 − 14)	16
Depreciation (this is given, but could be calculated, see Working 1, i.e. W1 below)	26
Profit and loss on sale of fixed assets	—
Interest paid (given)	9
Tax appropriated (given in the P&L A/c)	12
Dividend appropriated (given in the P&L A/c)	10
	73

Movements in current assets and current liabilities

	£000	
Stocks (up), i.e. more cash tied up	40	
Debtors (up)	15	
Creditors (down)	6	61
		12

You should note that the £73,000 figure above is the net profit before interest and tax (NPBIT) plus the depreciation added back, which could be computed as follows:

	£000
Net profit before tax (given)	38
Add Debenture interest (given)	9
Net profit before interest and tax	47
Add Depreciation	26
	73

☐ *Step 2*

Next, compute the amount which has been spent on the purchase of new fixed assets, as follows:

	Cost of land and buildings £000	Cost of plant and machinery £000
This year 19X8	320	152
Less Last year 19X7	280	130
	40	22

□ *Step 3*

You then pick up the whole of the sale proceeds for any fixed assets or investments which have been sold during the period, if any. In this example there weren't any.

□ *Step 4*

Then you pick up any new finance coming in such as share capital, loans or debentures, and borrowings repaid:

	This year 19X8 £000	Last year 19X7 £000	+ or − £000
Ordinary share capital	450	300	150
11% debentures	50	120	(70)

□ *Step 5*

Finally ensure that your calculations agree with the increase (or decrease) in the cash and bank balances:

	This year 19X8 £000	Last year 19X7 £000	+ or − £000
Cash at bank	20	14	6

This will provide you with an arithmetic check on the accuracy of your other figures.

WORKINGS

W1 The calculation of the depreciation charge for the year.

This was given as £26,000. However, if it is not given we compare the depreciation to date figures, as follows:

	Depreciation of plant and machinery £000
This year 19X8	50
Less Last year 19X7	24
= Charged in this year's P&L account	£26

However, this particular calculation will only suffice in cases where no sales of fixed assets have taken place, e.g. as in this example. We will look at how the sale of a fixed asset affects the figures which go into the funds flow/cash flow shortly.

EXAMPLE 8.3   Cash flow statement

Jean Ltd
Cash Flow Statement for the Year Ended (FRS 1) 31 December 19X8

	£000	£000
Net cash flow from operating activities		12
Returns on investments, and the servicing of finance		
Dividends received	—	
Dividends paid	(7)	
Interest paid	(9)	(16)
		(4)
Taxation		
Tax paid		(8)
		(12)
Investing activities		
Purchase of tangible fixed assets	(62)	
Sale of tangible fixed assets	—	
Proceeds from sale of trade investments	—	(62)
		(74)
Financing		
Proceeds from new share capital	150	
Repayment of borrowings	(70)	80
Increase in cash and cash equivalents		6

SELF-ASSESSMENT

Emmsock plc

From the information provided below see if you can prepare a cash flow statement by using the specimen blank FAS 1 layout, which follows the balance sheet and profit and loss appropriation account summary for Emmsock plc.

Emmsock plc
Balance sheet as at 31 December 19X7

Last year 19X6			Authorized share capital:	This year 19X7	
£000	£000			£000	£000
600			£1 ordinary shares	600	
200	800		10% preference shares	200	800

£000	£000	£000		£000	£000	£000
			Capital employed:			
			Issued share capital			
	200		Ordinary – issued/fully paid		400	
	—		10% preference shares		50	
		200				450
			Reserves			
	17		Share premium account		38	
	10		General reserve		15	
	20		Profit and loss account		45	
		47				98
		247	**Capital and reserves**			548
		165	8% debentures			100
		160	Loan			—
		£572				£648

	Depreciation		**Employment of capital**		Depreciation	
Cost	to date	Net	**Fixed assets**	Cost	to date	Net
£000	£000	£000		£000	£000	£000
450	—	450	Land and buildings	500	—	500
104	34	70	Plant and machinery	114	50	64
40	8	32	Fixtures and fittings	45	15	30
594	42	552		659	65	594

			Working capital			
			Current assets			
	27		Stock		33	
	31		Debtors		44	
	11		Bank		24	
	69		*Less* **Current liabilities**		101	
25			Creditors	14		
9			Taxation	13		
15	49	20	Proposed dividend	20	47	54
		£572				£648

Profit and loss appropriation account summary for year ended 31 December 19X7

	£000	£000
Net profit before tax*	65	
Less Corporation tax	15	50
Transfer to general reserve	5	
Proposed dividends	20	25
		25
Add Balance b/f from last year		20
Balance c/f (as per balance sheet)		£45

*After depreciation
Interest on debentures and loans charged in computing
   the profit amounted to   £22,000

When you have completed your attempt, then compare it with the answer which is provided on pages 183–6.

Emmsock plc
Cash flow statement for the year ended 31 December 19X7

(FRS 1 *layout*)	£000	£000
Net cash flow from operating activities		
Returns on investments, and the servicing of finance		
Dividends received		
Dividends paid		
Interest paid		
Taxation	—	—
Tax paid		
		—
Investing activities		
Purchase of tangible fixed assets		
Sale of tangible fixed assets		
Proceeds from sale of trade investments		
	—	—
Financing		
Proceeds from new share capital		
Repayment of borrowings		
	—	—
Increase or decrease in cash and cash equivalents		
		—

The sale of fixed assets

The sale of fixed assets makes the picture a little more complex and will be dealt with in the cash flow as follows:

☐ The profit or loss on sale will be adjusted for in the computation of the net cash flow from operating activities.

(a) a profit on sale, which could also be described as an over-provision for depreciation, must be deducted. This, in effect, takes the net profit before taxation back to what it was before the profit on sale was added;

(b) a loss on sale, i.e. an underprovision for depreciation, will be added back.

☐ The whole of the sale proceeds received must then be included in the investing activities section of the cash flow as illustrated in Figure 8.4.

☐ Care must be exercised when computing the cost of new fixed assets purchased during the period under review and when computing the depreciation for the period.

EXAMPLE 8.4   Sale of fixed assets

Plant and machinery	Cost	Depreciation to date	Net
	£000	£000	£000
19X3	300	70	230
19X4	440	86	354

During 19X4 a machine which cost £28,000 on which £17,000 depreciation had been charged, was sold for £12,000, thus:

	£000
Machine cost	28
Less depreciation	17
Book value	11
Sale proceeds	12
Profit on sale	1

The profit on sale of £1,000 would be deducted in the computation of the net cash flow from operating activities and the £12,000 sale proceeds would be included as a source of funds in the investing activities section. The new fixed assets purchased and the depreciation for the period can be calculated, as follows:

Plant and machinery	Cost	Depreciation to date
	£000	£000
Brought forward from 19X3	300	70
Less Applicable to machine sold	28	17
= Plant and machinery	272	53
b/f but not disposed of		
Carried forward 19X4	440	86

Cost of new plant and machinery = £168   Depreciation charged in 19X4 = £33

SELF-ASSESSMENT

Festiclyn plc (Cash flow)

Now see if you can prepare another cash flow statement in the FRS 1 format from the information provided for Festiclyn plc.

Festiclyn plc
Balance sheet summary

	19X7 31 December	19X8 31 December
	£000	£000
Capital employed:		
Ordinary shares £1 each	200	350
9% preference shares £1 each	120	nil
P&L account	40	55
Bank loan	nil	60
Trade creditors	25	29
Dividends payable	16	22
Taxation	64	78
	£465	£594
Represented by:		
Plant and machinery		
Cost	490	563
Aggregate depreciation	76	90
	414	473
Stock	21	75
Debtors	19	27
Bank	11	19
	£465	£594

You are also given the following summarized profit and loss appropriation account for the year ended 31 December 19X8:

	£000
Profit before tax (after depreciation)	109
Taxation:	
Corporation tax for the year	72
	37
Proposed dividend (ordinary shares)	22
	15
Balance b/f	40
	55

You are also informed that during the year ended 31 December 19X8 plant costing £24,000 on which £4,000 depreciation had been provided was sold for £17,000.

The profit before tax was after charging bank loan interest of £5,000. You will find the answer to this self check assessment on page 186.

What has happened to working capital?

This problem is solved by the now obsolete in accounting standard *SSAP 10* 'Statement of sources and applications of funds', as illustrated by Figure 8.5.

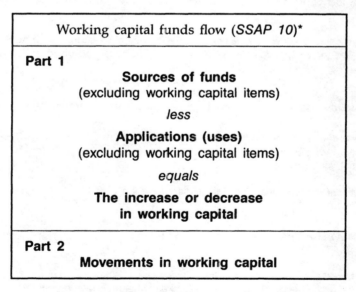

Figure 8.5 The working capital funds flow.

Its aim is to show how the financial resources have been used and the way in which the business has financed its operations. It may be obsolete for UK financial reporting purposes, but it is still a very useful way of looking at what has happened to the working capital. It should tell us whether or not the business is using its working capital to finance certain of its fixed assets. It will also show us the amount by which the working capital has gone up or down and how this is represented by the movements in the individual working capital items, such as stock, debtors, creditors, etc.

*In the United Kingdom, for financial reporting purposes the SSAP 10 funds flow has been replaced, for the time being, by the FRS 1 cash flow statement.

Preparing the working capital funds flow

EXAMPLE 8.5

As you work through each step see if you can tie it up with the information provided in the Jean Ltd example (Example 8.3) and the Jean Ltd statement of source and application of funds which follows.

☐ *Step 1*
  First, we must pick up the net profit before tax that has been earned during the period. We pick this up from the profit and loss account (extract), £38,000.

☐ *Step 2*
  Next, we need to know how much depreciation was charged in computing the net profit before tax, for the period. This you may recall that this was given in Example 8.2 as £26,000.

☐ *Step 3*
  Compare the issued share capital figures (and share premium figures, if any) as follows:

Issued ordinary share capital	£000
This year	450
Less Last year	300
= Additional ordinary share capital issued during the year	150

There is no share premium in the Jean Ltd example.

☐ *Step 4*
  Ignore the P&L account figures in the balance sheet. Why? Because the figure which we do need, i.e. the net profit before tax, has already been picked up from the profit and loss account (extract).

□ *Step 5*

Compare all other balance sheet figures including dividends and taxation but excluding other working capital items, using the following guidelines:

Sources of funds	**Applications**
Increase in a liability	Decrease in a liability
Decrease in an asset	Increase in an asset

Thus, the debentures decrease of £70,000 represents a repayment of debentures and is an application. The £40,000 additional land and buildings and the additional plant and machinery of £22,000, represents an application of funds, i.e. money going out. The £7,000 paid in dividends and the £8,000 paid in tax (note also the calculations which follow the Jean Ltd working capital funds flow) are also applications, W1.

□ *Step 6*

Complete the movements in the working capital section of this statement using the following as a guide:

Decreases in working capital	**Increases in working capital**
Decrease in current assets	Increase in current assets
Increase in current liabilities	Decrease in current liabilities

In Jean Ltd, stocks, debtors and the bank have all increased which increases the working capital. Creditors have decreased which also means an increase in working capital.

EXAMPLE 8.6   Explain movements in working capital, etc. to Jean Ltd (SSAP 10 format)

Jean Ltd
Statement of source and application of funds for the year ended 19X8 (funds flow)

	£000	£000
Source of funds		
Net profit before tax		38
Adjustment for items not involving the movement of funds		
(Add back) Depreciation (50 − 24)		26
Total generated from operations		64
Plus		
Funds from other sources		
Ordinary shares (450 − 300)		150
		214
Less **Application of funds**		
Repaid 11% debentures (50 − 120)	70	
Land and buildings (280 − 320)	40	
Plant and machinery (130 − 152)	22	
Dividend (see below)	7	
Taxation (see below)	8	
	—	147
		67
Increase/(decrease) in working capital:		
Stocks (50 − 90)	40	
Debtors (35 − 50)	15	
Creditors (36 − 30)	6	
Movement in net liquid funds:		
Bank (14 − 20)	6	67

WORKINGS

	Dividend £000	Taxation £000
Balance b/f (19X7)	7	8
Add Amount per P&L appropriation account	10	12
	17	20
Less Balance carried forward (19X8)	10	12
= Amount paid	7	8

SELF-ASSESSMENT

Festiclyn plc (Working Capital)

Using the Festiclyn plc information which you looked at earlier on in this chapter, now have a go at preparing a working capital funds flow using the work sheet provided below.

Festiclyn plc

Statement of source and application of funds for the year ended (*SSAP 10 Format*)

	£000	£000
Source of funds		
Net profit before tax		
Adjustment for items not involving the movement of funds:		
(Add back) Depreciation		
Total generated from operations		
Plus		
Funds from other sources		
Less **Application of funds**		
Increase/(decrease) in working capital:		
Stocks		
Debtors		
Creditors		
Movement in net liquid funds:		
Bank		
Cash		
Short-term investments		

Calculations required:
1. Taxation
2. Dividends

When you have completed this self-assessment, compare your answer with the suggested answer which is given on pages 188–9.

Funds flow statements: The essence

A knowledge of funds flow techniques will help answer questions such as:

- What has happened to cash?
- Why has profit gone up and cash gone down?
- Where have the profits gone?
- What has happened to the working capital?

In addition to showing the funds generated from operating activities during the period, a funds flow/cash flow statement will also show the other funds which were received during the period and what has become of them, i.e. the uses to which they have been put.

What has happened to cash?

Figure 8.2 explains the format of a funds flow which will help to illustrate what has happened to the cash/bank balances over a period of time.

The figures used to produce Figure 8.2 funds flow can be arrived at by comparing this year's balance sheet figures with last year's balance sheet figures, and adopting the following rules:

Sources of funds:
Increases in capital and liabilities.
Decreases in assets (other than cash/bank).
Depreciation of fixed assets (because it is a non-cash item).

Applications (uses) of funds:
Increases in assets (other than cash/bank).
Decreases in capital and liabilities.

equals
Increase/decrease in cash/bank balances for the period

However, certain figures which are needed for this funds flow may have to be calculated as follows, for example, dividends paid and tax paid (from the Jean Ltd example):

	Dividend £000	Taxation £000
Balance b/f (19X7) i.e. owing at start of year	7	8
Add P&L account appropriation (for 19X8)	10	12
	17	20
Less Balance c/f (19X8) i.e. owing at year end	10	12
= Amount paid	£7	£8

The FRS 1 cash flow statement
The funds flow statement which is currently being used for external reporting purposes in the United Kingdom, i.e. it forms part of the published accounts/company's annual report is the FRS 1 cash flow statement.

As with other funds flows it is a re-classification and re-ordering of profit and loss account and balance sheet data. It shows:

☐ *The net cash flow from operating activities*
You should note that this is made up of the net profit before interest and tax, plus depreciation of fixed assets, plus losses on the sale of fixed assets (or less profit), and then adjusted for movements in stocks, debtors and creditors (see Example 8.2).

☐ *Returns on investments (if any), and the cost of servicing the financing*
E.g. dividends paid to ordinary and preference shareholders, loan and debenture interest, etc.

☐ *Taxation*
You should note the way in which we calculated the tax-paid figure.

☐ *Investing activities*
The purchase and sale of fixed assets, etc.

☐ *Financing*
Details of new finance, e.g. more ordinary share capital and also details of repayments of loans and debentures, etc.

The final figure should then be equal to the increase or decrease in the cash and bank balances.

The sale of fixed assets

If a fixed asset (or an investment) is sold during the period under review note the treatment for cash flow/funds flow purposes in example 8.3 and the Festiclyn plc self-assessment, and Figure 8.5 which follows.

What has happened to working capital?

The answer to this question is provided by the *SSAP 10* 'Statement of source and application of funds (funds flow)'. Figure 8.5 shows that the statement simply consists of four sections:

1. Funds from trading operations.
2. Funds from other sources.
3. The application (uses) of funds.
4. Movements in working capital.

Section 1:
Funds from trading operations:
Net profit before tax
Add back depreciation
Add back loss on sale of assets
Less profit on sale of assets

Section 2:
Add funds from other sources
e.g. Increase in loans; proceeds from the sale of fixed assets

---

Section 3:
Less application of funds
e.g. Dividends paid, tax paid
     New fixed assets purchased

Section 4:
= Increase or decrease in working capital

Figure 8.6 *SSAP 10* – the source and application of funds.

If a fixed asset (or an investment) is sold during the period under review the treatment for funds flow purposes will be as illustrated in Figure 8.6 opposite.

□ In section 1, funds from trading operations, the following will apply:
   (a) a loss on sale will be added back;
   (b) a profit on sale will be deducted.

The profit or loss on sale is the difference between the sale proceeds and the book value (i.e. cost less depreciation) of an asset. It is not a cash profit or loss. It can in fact be regarded as either an underprovision or overprovision for depreciation, i.e.:
   (a) a loss on sale equals an underprovision for depreciation;
   (b) a profit on sale equals an overprovision for depreciation.

□ In section 2, funds from other sources, the whole of the sale proceeds from the sale of fixed assets will be included.

□ The calculation of depreciation for section 1 and the cost of new fixed assets purchased for section 3, application of funds must take into account the cost and depreciation to date of any fixed assets sold, as follows (extract from the Festiclyn plc self-assessment):

Fixed asset	Cost £000	Depreciation to date £000
Plant:		
Brought forward at the start of the year (19X7)	490	76
Less Plant sold	24	4
Plant held at start of year, which is still held at the end of the year	466	72
Balance, carried forward at the end of the year (19X8)	563	90
19X8 funds flow information	**£97**	**£18**

Please note that a cash flow forecast (cash budget) is a different kind of financial statement and is not another name for a cash flow statement or a funds flow. Should you wish to know more about the cash flow forecast/cash budgets please consult *The Essence of Management Accounting* which is also in this series.

Thus, a funds flow is a statement which is prepared in addition to the trading and profit and loss account and the balance sheet, showing the manner in which a business has financed its operations.

Further reading

Dyson, J., *Accounting for Non-Accounting Students* (Pitman, 1994).

Edwards, J. R. and Mellett, H. J., *Introduction to Accounting* (Paul Chapman Publishing, 1995).

9

Ratio analysis: the interpretation of financial statements

Objectives

This chapter is really the heart and essence of this book. You should now be reasonably familiar with the principal accounting statements and the concepts on which they are based.

When you have completed this chapter you should be able to look at financial statements, i.e. the trading and profit and loss accounts and the balance sheets, and be able to do the following:

□ Calculate the ratios illustrated.

□ Appreciate who is interested in them.

□ Understand what they are trying to measure.

□ Know what is meant by value added, and how a value added statement is laid out.

□ Identify the requirements for effective ratio analysis/interfirm comparison.

□ Prepare a ratio analysis using the working notes system.

□ Appreciate the limitations of ratio analysis.

Accounting ratios

Why use ratios?

Ratio analysis is the tool by which we attempt to measure and compare financial performance. However, you must appreciate from the outset that

117

the accounting ratios on their own are pretty meaningless. They should be looked at in conjunction with other data and not in isolation. Three of the principal reasons for using ratio analysis are:

☐ To identify areas in which the company needs to carry out further investigations/studies.
☐ To pin-point the areas in which the company may improve its performance or would appear to have a differential advantage over its competitors.
☐ To provoke questions.

However, you must remember that when it comes to intercompany (interfirm) comparisons the ratios will be meaningless unless you compare like with like. The source data must have been arrived at using similar accounting policies and the ratios computed in the same way.

Which ratios?

Ratio analysis is a minefield. There are numerous ratios, conflicting opinions, a vast amount of terminology and calculation variations.

The ratios which we advocate here are just a small selection of the ratios which can be used. However, they should provide you with a good foundation/framework with which to interpret and assess the financial performance of a company or companies. Ratios may be classified in a number of ways; we will group them as follows:

☐ *Profitability*
This helps you to answer questions such as:
(a) am I getting a satisfactory return on my investment?
(b) are we getting a good return on all of the capital which has been invested in the business?

☐ *Liquidity*
This is all about the company's ability to pay its way in the world of business and the management of its working capital.

☐ *Efficiency*
This looks at the way in which the company uses its assets.

☐ *Capital structure*
This is about the composition and relationship which exist between the equity (i.e. the ordinary share capital or the ordinary share capital plus

reserves) and the other long-term sources of finance, such as preference shares, debentures, long-term loans, etc.

□ *Employee*
This is used to assess the efficiency with which the labour force is being used.

□ *Investment*
This takes a look at the financial performance of the company's shares.

We will now take a more in-depth view of each group. We will provide you with an indication as to why the ratios are used, who uses them and how they are calculated. To illustrate the calculations in a practical way we will use the data provided in Figure 9.1 relating to Linboo plc. Note that, throughout, all of the calculations are in £000s.

Profitability ratios

Gross profit to sales
This is of great interest to the management of the company and also the tax authorities. It indicates the average mark-up on the products/services which have been sold during the period. When you are dealing in thousands of pounds, a small percentage increase or decrease in the gross margin (mark-up) can have a significant impact upon the profits.

Figure 9.2 gives a worked example of gross profit to sales which is calculated as follows:

$$\frac{\text{Gross profit}}{\text{Sales}} \times 100$$

Possible reasons for the fall of 5% shown in Figure 9.2 could be the following:

□ A reduction in selling prices.
□ An increase in the cost of raw materials.
□ An increase in carriage inwards, i.e. the carriage paid on materials purchased.
□ Stock losses due to pilferage, poor storage or obsolescence.
□ Stocktaking errors, e.g. pricing errors, or stock simply being omitted from the stocktaking sheets.

Figure 9.1 shows an abridged version of the accounts of Linboo plc.

Linboo plc
Trading account and profit and loss account year ended 31 October

(£000s)		19X4		19X5
Sales		2,500		3,200
Less Cost of sales		1,500		2,080
Gross profit		1,000		1,120
Less Expenses (including debenture interest				
and depreciation)		750		720
Net profit before tax		250		400
Corporation tax		50		92
Net profit after tax		200		308
Less Dividend (paid and proposed)		30		48
		170		260
Balance b/f	(19×3)	430	(19×4)	600
		£600		£860

Balance sheet as at 31 October

		19X4		19X5
Ordinary share capital (in £1 shares)		300		500
Share premium account		–		140
Retained earnings (P&L account balance)		600		860
		900		1,500
Long-term debt:				
12% debenture		300		150
Capital employed		**£1,200**		**£1,650**
Fixed assets:				
Cost		750		1,540
Depreciation		170		340
WDV	(A)	£580		£1,200
Current assets:	19×3			
Stock	240	300		290
Debtors	320	250		420
Bank		230		40
	(B)	780		750
Less Current liabilities:	19×3			
Trade creditors	145	135	265	
Proposed dividend	25	160 (C)	35	300 (C)
Net worth (A) + (B) − (C)		**£1,200**		**£1,650**

Other information
Market price per share		£1.50	£1.80
		£000	£000
Interest paid (included in the calculation			
of the net profit before tax)		36	18
Purchases		1,560	2,070

Figure 9.1 Financial data of Linboo plc.

19X4	19X5
$\dfrac{£1,000}{£2,500} \times 100 = 40\%$	$\dfrac{£1,120}{£3,200} \times 100 = 35\%$

Figure 9.2 Gross profits to sales ratio.

19X4	19X5
$\dfrac{£250}{£2,500} \times 100 = 10\%$ i.e. £10 for every £100 of sales	$\dfrac{£400}{£3,200} \times 100 = 12.5\%$ i.e. £12.50 for every £100 of sales

Figure 9.3 Net profits to sales ratio.

Net profit to sales (net margin)

In addition to the factors which affect the gross profit, the net profit/sales percentage is affected by what is happening to the overhead expenses and depreciation.

Figure 9.3 gives a worked example of the net profit to sales ratio which is calculated as follows:

$$\frac{\text{Net profit before tax}}{\text{Sales}} \times 100$$

Again, this will be useful for management because it helps them to keep a watchful eye on their overhead expenses.

The increase in the net profit/sales percentage seen in Figure 9.3 could be caused by a variety of factors, which reduce the overhead expenditure, such as the following:

☐ Moving premises to an area where rents and/or business rates are lower.

☐ Changes in the company's policy of financing fixed assets, e.g. renting or leasing fixed assets.

☐ Changes in the company's depreciation policy.

☐ A reduction in bad debts and/or the provision for bad debts.

☐ Less interest to pay on debentures. In Linboo plc debenture interest went down to half its 19X4 level in 19X5.

19X4	19X5
$\dfrac{£250 + £36}{£1,200} \times 100 = 23.84\%$	$\dfrac{£400 + £18}{£1,650} \times 100 = 25.34\%$

Figure 9.4 Return on investment (ROI) ratio.

□ The shedding of personnel, i.e. a reduction in the labour force and/or working less overtime.

□ Creative accounting, e.g. carrying forward significant stocks of stationery to the next accounting period, prepaid advertising, etc.

Return on investment

Return on investment (ROI) can also be called return on capital employed (ROCE) and return on assets.

Financial management is particularly concerned with the productivity of all the capital employed. Thus, companies like to have an overall indication of the productivity of all their capital. The following ratio should satisfy this need:

$$\frac{\text{Net profit before tax} + \text{loan and debenture interest}}{\text{Capital employed (less intangibles, if any)}} \times 100$$

or in other words:

$$\frac{\text{Net profit before interest and tax (NPBIT)}}{\text{Capital employed (less intangibles, if any)}} \times 100$$

This ratio is demonstrated in Figure 9.4. The debenture interest was added back so that the ratio could show the return on all capital, irrespective of where it came from. Business is about investing money in it, putting that money to work, and then being able to generate a satisfactory return for those who have provided it.

Other authors may use net profit before tax or net profit after tax over capital employed. Also note that capital employed equals ordinary share capital plus reserves, plus preference share capital (if any), plus long-term loans and debentures. Capital employed can also equal total assets less intangibles, less current liabilities, i.e. the net tangible assets (net worth less intangibles) should in the majority of cases give the same figure.

The reasons for an improvement (or deterioration) in this ratio are those factors which explain the gross profit/sales percentage and net profit/sales percentage plus movements in share capital, reserves and long-term debt.

19X4	19X5
$$\frac{£780}{£160} = 4.88$$ i.e. for every £1 owing to current liabilities they have £4.88 cover	$$\frac{£750}{£300} = 2.50$$ i.e. for every £1 owing to current liabilities they have £2.50 cover

Figure 9.5 The current ratio.

Liquidity ratios

Liquidity ratios are important to the management, shareholders, lenders and creditors because liquidity ratios provide a measure of the company's ability to pay its debts. A company can be quite profitable but still have liquidity problems. Profitability and liquidity do not go hand in hand. The ratios should provide an indication of whether or not the company has liquidity problems or excess liquidity.

The current ratio
The current ratio (or ratio of current assets/current liabilities) is given as follows:

$$\frac{\text{Current assets}}{\text{Current liabilities}}$$

A worked example of the current ratio is shown in Figure 9.5.

It is difficult to comment on Figure 9.5 without a yardstick. So, assuming that the industry average is 2:1, it would appear that last year (19X4) Linboo plc had excess liquidity. However, it is quite likely that this was used to redeem debentures and/or invest in new fixed assets in 19X5, because the bank balance appeared to be high at £230,000.

The acid test
The acid test (or quick) ratio is expressed as follows:

$$\frac{\text{Liquid assets (i.e. current assets less stocks)}}{\text{Current liabilities}}$$

As a rule of thumb, this ratio should be around 1.00 (i.e. one to one). However, many industries work on less than one to one. If, in the example shown in Figure 9.6, the industry averages for the two years were 0.90 for 19X4, and 0.85 for 19X5, then clearly the picture portrayed by the ratios of 3.00 and 1.54, respectively, signifies excess liquidity.

19X4	19X5
$\dfrac{£780 - £300}{£160} = 3.00$	$\dfrac{£750 - £290}{£300} = 1.54$
i.e. for every £1 owing to current liabilities the company has £3 cover	i.e. for every £1 owing to current liabilities the company has £1.54 cover

Figure 9.6 The acid test ratio.

Efficiency ratios

The ratios which are grouped under this heading can also be referred to as activity ratios or asset utilization ratios. They are of particular interest to management/analysts because they provide a measure of how efficiently the company is managing its assets and working capital.

The average collection period

This credit control ratio provides an indication of how long it is taking the company to collect its debts. It is, therefore, of particular importance to those who are involved in the company's financial management. The ratio is expressed as follows:

$$\frac{\text{Average debtors}}{\text{Sales}} \times 365 = \text{Average collection period in days}$$

Average debtors are last year's balance sheet debtors plus this year's balance sheet debtors, divided by two.

From the example shown in Figure 9.7 it can be seen that Linboo plc's credit control has improved, the money owing from debtors is coming in that little bit quicker in 19X5 than in 19X4. If the industry average is 60 days, which is not untypical, then the company's credit control function would appear to be doing its job.

The credit period taken

Creditors, from whom goods and services have been purchased on credit, are a source of short-term finance. Financial managers will be interested in this ratio to see if they are paying off their debts too slowly or too quickly when compared with industry figures. The creditors will be interested in the figure so that they can compare it with the time it is taking the company to pay their amounts owing. Two example calculations follow:

$$\square \quad \frac{\text{Average creditors}}{\text{Sales}} \times 365 = \text{Credit period taken in days}$$

19X4	19X5
(£000)	(£000)
Average debtors = $\dfrac{320 + 250}{2}$	Average debtors = $\dfrac{250 + 420}{2}$
= 285	= 335
$\dfrac{285}{2,500} \times 365 = 42$ days (rounded up)	$\dfrac{335}{3,200} \times 365 = 39$ days (rounded up)

Figure 9.7 Debt collection (average collection period) ratio.

□ $\dfrac{\text{Average creditors}}{\text{Purchases}} \times 365 = $ Credit period taken in days

Average creditors are last year's balance sheet creditors plus this year's balance sheet creditors divided by two.

The second of the two calculations is the more realistic of the two. However, if the purchases figure is not available, then you have no choice but to use the sales figure. The purchases of Linboo plc were £1,560 for 19X4 and £2,070 for 19X5 (both £000), from the data provided in Figure 9.1.

If the industry average is 45 days, it would appear from the data in Figure 9.8 that the company is paying off its debts too quickly. However, if this is to secure generous cash discounts for prompt payment it may not be such a bad idea after all as a small percentage discount does have a high annual percentage rate (APR).

Stock turnover
Stock turnover is also known as 'stock turn', and it shows the number of times which the average stock held is sold in a given period. Stock does represent capital tied up, so it is preferable to have a rapid rate of stock turnover to ensure that it is tied up for a minimum amount of time. The average stock is computed by dividing the opening stock plus the closing stock of the period by two. Two example calculations follow:

□ $\dfrac{\text{Sales}}{\text{Average stocks}} = $ The rate of stock turnover

□ $\dfrac{\text{Cost of sales}}{\text{Average stocks}} = $ The rate of stock turnover

19X4	19X5
(£000)	(£000)
Average creditors $= \dfrac{145 + 135}{2}$	Average creditors $= \dfrac{135 + 265}{2}$
$= 140$	$= 200$
(a) $\dfrac{140}{2,500} \times 365 = 21$ days	(a) $\dfrac{200}{3,200} \times 365 = 23$ days
Using the purchases figure:	Using the purchases figure:
(b) $\dfrac{140}{1,560} \times 365 = 33$ days	(b) $\dfrac{200}{2,070} \times 365 = 36$ days

Figure 9.8 Finance from creditors (credit period taken) ratio.

The second of the two calculations is the more realistic of the two because stocks are valued at their cost price or lower. However, because the cost of sales information is not always available the first calculation is used quite extensively.

If we divide the rate of stock turnover by 365, it tells us the average time for which the stock is held before being sold. Using the figures from calculation (a) in Figure 9.9 the position is as follows:

☐ For 19X4: $\dfrac{365}{9.26} = 40$ days (rounded up)

☐ For 19X5: $\dfrac{365}{10.85} = 34$ days (rounded up)

The higher the rate of turnover, the smaller the period of time for which stock is being carried. Thus, the above figures illustrate that the position has improved, i.e. stock is being tied up for a shorter period of time.

This means that there is also likely to be lower wastage caused by deterioration and obsolescence. A rapid rate of turnover equals fast-moving stock and less capital tied up.

Sales to fixed assets

This ratio provides a measure of asset utilization. It should be treated with caution when attempting to carry out an interfirm comparison. This is because companies may rent or lease a lot of their fixed assets. Fixed assets

19X4	19X5
(£000)	(£000)
Average stock $= \dfrac{240 + 300}{2} = 270$	Average stock $= \dfrac{300 + 290}{2} = 295$
(a) $\dfrac{2,500}{270} = 9.26$ times	(a) $\dfrac{3,200}{295} = 10.85$ times
(b) $\dfrac{1,500}{270} = 5.56$ times	(b) $\dfrac{2,080}{295} = 7.05$ times

Figure 9.9 The rate of turnover (stock turn) ratio.

which are rented or leased (other than leasehold property) do not appear in the balance sheet, they are 'off balance sheet' financing.

A decision also has to be taken as to which fixed assets should be included in the ratio. Should we include all of the fixed assets or just the manufacturing fixed assets?

Thus, we can calculate it in a number of ways, two of which are as follows:

☐ $\dfrac{\text{Sales}}{\text{Fixed assets}}$

☐ $\dfrac{\text{Sales}}{\text{Manufacturing fixed assets}}$

Note that there is insufficient information provided in Figure 9.1 for Linboo plc from which to calculate this ratio.

According to the figures shown in Figure 9.10 the company became less efficient in 19X5 generating a lower sales figure per £1 invested in fixed assets. However, the dramatic increase in fixed assets may not have taken place until towards the end of 19X5 and therefore, the benefit of the new investment should have an impact on next year's performance. On the other hand, the company could have been caught out by a downturn in the economy.

Capital structure (gearing) ratios

Gearing (or leverage) is all about the relationship between the equity, i.e. ordinary share capital plus reserves, and *the other forms of long-term financing*, including preference shares, long-term loans, debentures, and if circumstances warrant it the bank overdraft.

19X4	19X5
(a)	**(a)**
$\dfrac{2,500}{580} = 4.31$	$\dfrac{3,200}{1,200} = 2.67$
i.e. generating £4.31 of sales for every £1 invested in fixed assets	i.e. generating £2.67 of sales for every £1 invested in fixed assets

Figure 9.10 Sales to fixed assets ratio.

A company which has a high proportion of the other forms of long-term financing is referred to as being **high geared**. A company with a low proportion of the other forms of long-term financing is said to be **low geared**. In the event of adverse trading conditions it is the more highly geared companies which suffer, because of their obligations to make interest payments/repayments of capital on long-term loans and debentures. It is of particular importance to the company's financial management and the external providers of capital.

Gearing (leverage)
Examples of gearing ratios are as follows:

1. $\dfrac{\text{Debt, i.e. other forms of long-term financing (excluding the bank overdraft)}}{\text{Debt (excluding the bank overdraft)} + \text{Ordinary share capital} + \text{reserves}} \times 100$

2. As above, but including the bank overdraft

3. $\dfrac{\text{Debt}}{\text{Equity (i.e. issued ordinary shares} + \text{reserves)}}$

This is also called the Debt/Equity Ratio or Borrowings/Ordinary Shareholders' Funds.

From the example shown in Figure 9.11, it can be seen that the gearing for Linboo plc has gone down significantly during 19X5 because some of the debentures have been redeemed and new ordinary share capital and share premium have been introduced. To make a more informed comment you need to look at industry figures. What is high or low geared will depend upon the industry in which the company operates, e.g. below the industry average could be classed as low, above could be classed as high.

19X4	19X5
(£000)	(£000)
(a) $\dfrac{300}{1,200} \times 100 = 25\%$	(a) $\dfrac{150}{1,650} \times 100 = 9.09\%$

Figure 9.11 Gearing ratio (using the example 1 calculation).

Why include the bank overdraft? If the company is using its bank overdraft as a long-term source of funds, then it should, quite rightly, be included in the gearing calculation.

If, and when, you see other gearing ratios, remember the following:

□ Equity = issued ordinary share capital plus reserves, i.e. ordinary shareholders' funds.
□ Net worth = capital employed.
□ Net worth = total assets less current liabilities, i.e. the net assets.
□ Net worth = ordinary shareholders' funds plus the other forms of long-term financing.
□ Net worth = net assets.

Be warned that there are many more gearing ratios. However, they are all trying to say something similar, about the relationship which exists between the equity and the other sources of long-term funds.

Some analysts/writers include preference shares with the long-term debt, others add it on to the equity. The reason for this conflict of opinion, is that preference shares do not carry as high a risk to the company as do long-term loans and debentures, i.e. the obligation to make interest payments/repayments by stated dates. It is possible to defer paying a preference dividend should the company so decide. However, a company cannot defer a payment of interest to debenture holders. To default on making loan repayments could be a very perilous manoeuvre!

Interest cover
This is an income-based measure of gearing. It is of interest to the company's financial management and long-term lenders, such as debenture holders, bankers, etc. It shows how well the company can cover their interest payments, and is calculated as follows:

$$\frac{\text{Net profit before interest and tax (NPBIT)}}{\text{Loan and debenture interest}}$$

19X4	19X5
(£000) Net profit before tax　　250 *Add back* Debenture interest　36 NPBIT　　286 $\dfrac{286}{36}$ = 7.95 times	(£000) Net profit before tax　　400 *Add back* Debenture interest　18 NPBIT　　418 $\dfrac{418}{18}$ = 23.23 times

Figure 9.12 Interest cover ratio.

It can be observed from a review of Figure 9.12 that the reduction in the gearing, coupled with the increase in profits, has made a dramatic improvement in the interest cover. Because of their low gearing and increased investment in fixed assets (i.e. additional security), Linboo plc are in a very good position to raise further debt capital, i.e. long-term loans and debentures, should they need more finance.

If we include the preference dividend in the calculation, the ratio then becomes known as **the fixed charge cover**, the calculation being as follows:

$$\frac{\text{Net profit before interest and tax}}{\text{Loan interest plus debenture interest plus preference dividend}}$$

Employee ratios

Employee ratios tend to be used in an attempt to assess the productivity and efficiency of the labour force. Again, care has to be exercised when carrying out interfirm comparisons to take account of the degree of mechanization and use of robotics, and the location, for instance, wage rates for the same type of work could be higher or lower in other parts of the United Kingdom and in Europe.

Four types of employee ratios are detailed as follows:

1. Average remuneration per employee:

$$\frac{\text{Total wages/salaries paid to employees for the year}}{\text{Average number of employees on the payroll}}$$

2. Net profit per employee:

$$\frac{\text{Net profit before tax}}{\text{Average number of employees on the payroll}}$$

3. Sales per employee:

$$\frac{\text{Sales}}{\text{Average number of employees on the payroll}}$$

4. Directors' efficiency:

$$\frac{\text{Directors' remuneration (salaries, fees, etc.)}}{\text{Net profit before tax} + \text{directors' remuneration}} \times 100$$

The fourth of these ratios shows the directors' earnings as a percentage of the profits generated after adding back their earnings, which is useful for interfirm comparisons and trade unions. Why a directors' efficiency ratio? Directors are responsible for the success of their company, especially when it comes to the bottom line, i.e. the profit or loss.

Investment ratios

This group of ratios looks at financial performance of the company relating to the ordinary shares. The financial management, existing ordinary shareholders, would-be investors, analysts and competitors will all be very interested in these ratios.

Earnings/shareholders' equity (return on equity)

The earnings/shareholders' equity (or return on equity) ratio is a measure of the return on investment applicable to the ordinary shareholders. It is computed as follows:

$$\frac{\text{Net profit after tax less preference dividend (if any)}}{\text{Equity, i.e. issued ordinary share capital plus reserves}} \times 100$$

This ratio helps answer the question asked by ordinary shareholders of, what is in it for me? The ratio looks at what is left for the ordinary shareholders after paying/providing for the business expenses, including debenture and loan interest, directors' remuneration, taxation and preference dividends. Thus, it is in fact a ratio which reflects the self interest of the ordinary shareholders, i.e. the equity shareholders.

The decrease in the figures shown in Figure 9.13 is probably due to the

19X4	19X5
$\dfrac{200}{900} \times 100 = 22.23\%$	$\dfrac{308}{1,500} \times 100 = 20.54\%$

Figure 9.13 Earnings/shareholders' ratio.

new and significant investment in fixed assets, which should benefit future accounting periods.

Dividend yield (on ordinary shares)
The dividend yield ratio simply relates the dividend to the market price of an ordinary share. However, it does give some idea to a potential investor of the expected rate of return on investment in terms of cash paid out. The ratio is expressed as follows:

$$\frac{\text{Dividend per share}}{\text{Market price per ordinary share}} \times 100$$

A worked example for Linboo plc is shown in Figure 9.14.

19X4	19X5
£000 £000	£000 £000
Dividend per share = 30 ÷ 300 = 0.10	Dividend per share = 48 ÷ 500 = 0.096
$\dfrac{£0.10}{£1.50} \times 100 = 6.67\%$	$\dfrac{£0.096}{£1.80} \times 100 = 5.34\%$
i.e. generating £6.67 for every £100 invested at the share price concerned	i.e. generating £5.34 for every £100 invested at the share price concerned

Figure 9.14 The dividend yield ratio.

However, the question of which share price to use is debatable. Should it be the share price at the start or end of the period, or an average covering the whole of the period? Because share prices fluctuate a lot it is perhaps fairer that an average is used. Thus the return calculated gives the return on the average value of the shares for the period.

19X4	19X5
$\dfrac{£200}{300}$ = £0.67 per share	$\dfrac{£308}{500}$ = £0.62 per share

Figure 9.15 Earnings per ordinary share ratio.

Earnings per ordinary share
The earnings per ordinary share ratio is also called the earnings per share (EPS) ratio and is expressed as follows:

$$\frac{\text{Net profit after tax less preference dividend (if any)}}{\text{Number of ordinary shares issued}}$$

The EPS is a measure of the earning power of each share and is closely linked to the share's market value. Thus, it shows the amount generated per share for the period (see Figure 9.15). Usually, a portion will be paid out as dividends and the balance ploughed back. This leads us into our next ratio, dividend cover.

Dividend cover
The dividend cover ratio shows the number of times that the current earnings cover the ordinary dividend which has been paid and/or proposed. It can be calculated as follows:

$$\frac{\text{Earnings per share}}{\text{Dividend per share}}$$

or using the totals:

$$\frac{\text{Net profit after tax less preference dividend}}{\text{Total ordinary share dividend}}$$

Thus, it could be said that this ratio provides an indication of the likelihood that the company will be able to maintain its dividends while being able to enjoy a healthy plough back of profits. A worked example of this ratio for Linboo plc is shown in Figure 9.16.

The price earnings ratio
A high price earnings (PE) ratio means a high price in relation to earnings. This possibly reflects market expectations of great things to come, i.e. a bright future is forecast.

19X4	19X5
$\dfrac{£0.67}{0.10} = 6.7$ times	$\dfrac{£0.62}{0.096} = 6.46$ times
i.e. for every £1 needed to pay the dividend £6.70 has been generated	i.e. for every £1 needed to pay the dividend £6.46 has been generated

Figure 9.16 Dividend cover ratio.

A low PE implies a low price in relation to earnings. The reason for this could be low expectations on the part of the market. However, entrepreneurs have been known to take over companies with low PEs and over a period of two to five years perform a turnaround and then sell them, making millions of pounds in the process.

The price earnings ratio is calculated as follows:

$$\frac{\text{Market price per ordinary share}}{\text{Earnings per ordinary share}}$$

This is the most commonly accepted relationship between a company's ability to generate profits and the market price of its ordinary shares.

The higher PE in 19X5 shown in Figure 9.17 could be attributable to an increase in market expectations of anticipated good results in the future, possibly as the new investment in fixed assets begins to bear fruit.

The inversion of this ratio provides a ratio known as the **capitalization rate** (or earnings yield), the rate at which the market is capitalizing the value of current earnings and is expressed as follows:

$$\frac{\text{Earnings per ordinary share}}{\text{Market price per ordinary share}} \times 100$$

As with the dividend yield, this ratio also gives an indication of the return on investment (ROI), i.e. return on capital/an indication of the cost of the equity share capital. A worked example of this for Linboo plc is shown in Figure 9.18. These ratios can be compared to those of other similar-sized companies within the same industrial sector.

Value added statements

The value added approach is an alternative way of looking at the information provided in the profit and loss account. Value added is the

19X4	19X5
$\dfrac{£1.50}{£0.67} = 2.24$ times	$\dfrac{£1.80}{£0.62} = 2.91$ times

Figure 9.17 The price earnings (PE) ratio.

19X4	19X5
$\dfrac{£0.67}{1.50} \times 100 = 44.67\%$	$\dfrac{£0.62}{1.80} \times 100 = 34.45\%$

Figure 9.18 The capitalization rate (or earnings yield) ratio.

difference between the amount we receive from sales and the materials and services which we buy from external suppliers. Thus, value added represents the additional wealth created by the company's own efforts through the application of its labour force, and its resources such as plant, machinery and equipment.

The value added statement (see Figure 9.19) shows how the value added has been arrived at and how it is shared out between the stakeholders. The stakeholders of a company are the following:

□ The employees (including directors) for their remuneration.
□ The providers of capital, for example, interest payments on loans and debentures, and dividends to preference and ordinary shareholders.
□ The government for taxation.
□ The company, by means of depreciation of fixed assets and retained earnings which are reinvested in the business.

Thus there are a number of ratios which can be used which look at relationships with value added, for example:

□ Value added per employee:

$$\frac{\text{Value added}}{\text{Number of employees}}$$

Value added statement

£000

Sales

Less Materials and services bought from outside suppliers
　　= **Value added**　　　　　　　　　　　　　　　　　———

Add Other income, e.g. investment income　　　　　　———
　　　　Value added available　　　　　　　　　　═══

Shared out between the stakeholders as follows:
　　Employees' remuneration
　　Debenture and loan interest
　　Preference shares
　　Ordinary shares
　　Taxation
　　Depreciation
　　Retained earnings

　　　　　　　　　　　　　　　　　　　　　　　　　———

　　　　　　　　　　　　　　　　　　　　　　　　　———

Note that 'other income' would also have to be accounted for in the statement.

Figure 9.19 The value added statement.

A measure of the productivity of labour.

□ Value added/input:

$$\frac{\text{Value added}}{\text{Materials and services from external sources}} = \frac{\text{Value added}}{\text{per £ of input}}$$

The extent to which the original input has grown.

□ Value added/manufacturing fixed assets

$$\frac{\text{Value added}}{\text{Manufacturing fixed assets}} = \frac{\text{Value added generated per £ of}}{\text{manufacturing fixed assets}}$$

Provides a measure of plant utilization.

□ Value added/capital employed

$$\frac{\text{Value added}}{\text{Capital employed}} = \text{Value added per £ of capital employed}$$

Gives an indication of the productivity of capital.

Using the information

The information which is generated can be presented using a comparative statement which could be drawn up on the lines of Figure 9.20. The

Ratio	This year 19X2	Last year 19X1	Reasons for variances/comments, e.g. strengths and weaknesses
Turnover	£531 m	£452 m	
Profit before tax	£38 m	£24 m	
Earnings per share	24.4p	11.75p	
Dividend cover	3.0 times	1.4 times	

Figure 9.20 Suggested layout for the comparative statement.

statement illustrated in Figure 9.20 includes a working notes column at the right-hand side reserved for explanations of reasons for variances and comments.

The comparative statement could also include an assortment of data and ratios covering the following:

☐ liquidity;

☐ profitability;

☐ capital structure; etc.

The format used in Figure 9.20 could also be used to compare two different companies, e.g. company A compared with company B, instead of this year/last year as shown.

Having made the working notes during the course of the analysis, the principal findings could then be summarized in a conclusions section together with any recommendations. Look at Figure 9.21 and see if you can spot the year in which Zimte plc experienced difficulties, i.e. a year which looks out of line when compared to other years.

You should have observed that the year 19X3 was out of line and, yes, the company did encounter problems in that year. What were the problems? On the current ratio the company only had £89 of current assets to cover every £100 of current liabilities which it owed. The acid test position had also deteriorated significantly. For every £100 owing to its current liabilities, the company only had £45 worth of cover in terms of its liquid assets. However, its average collection period, i.e. the speed at which it collects its debts in from debtors, improved. This could be due to the adverse liquidity position in which it found itself. If you are short of cash you are encouraged to collect your outstanding debts more quickly. This trend has continued and currently in year 19X6 the company is, on average, taking around 45 days to collect its debts. Also, you can see from the figures that since 19X3, the problem year, the company has improved its liquidity position.

The important message of Figure 9.21 concerning financial analysis is

	19X1	19X2	19X3	19X4	19X5	19X6
Zimte plc						
Liquidity						
Current ratio	1.34	1.65	0.89	1.13	1.32	1.40
Acid test	0.69	0.91	0.45	0.55	0.65	0.85
Debtors' average collection						
period (months)	2.30	1.90	1.70	1.60	1.50	1.50

Figure 9.21 Suggested layout for company financial analysis.

	Motor Component Industry		
Company	S	T	U
Year end	Dec 19X6	July 19X6	Dec 19X6
Ratio:	%	%	%
Return on capital employed	17.0	17.5	19.1
Profit margin	6.3	8.5	8.3
Average collection period	4.4	5.0	4.6
Gearing	47.7	32.8	39.1
Interest cover	6.1	7.1	6.4
Current ratio	1.8	1.8	1.7
Acid test	0.9	1.0	0.8

Figure 9.22 Industry figures – motor components.

that you need at least five or six years' worth of figures to be in a position to make a more realistic appraisal, e.g. the identification of trends. It is difficult to make sound judgements simply on the basis of a two-year analysis.

A comparison of ratios, one year with another for the same company, does not indicate whether the performance was good, bad or indifferent. Hence, the quest for a yardstick, i.e. a standard against which performance can be measured. The yardsticks which can be used are industry figures, either by comparing with other companies in the same area which are of a similar nature or by looking at industry averages. A wealth of this type of information is available on computer databases and in numerous publications. However, it is not always an easy task to carry out; for example company T in Figure 9.22 has a different year end to the other companies. Thus, the comparison does not cover the same trading period.

SELF-ASSESSMENTS

This chapter has provided you with the ratios, i.e. the tools, with which you can analyze and assess company performance. There now follow three separate self-assessments for you to use to check your understanding of the ratios. They are as follows:

□ Thirstin Leas Ltd.
□ Woodcroft plc.
□ Nether Ltd and Thong Ltd.

When you have completed each of the self-assessments compare your attempt with the suggested answers which you will find on page 189 onwards.

SELF-ASSESSMENT

Thirstin Leas Ltd

Trading and profit and loss account for the year
ended 31 December 19X2

	£000	£000
Sales		500
Less **Cost of sales:**		
Stock at 1 January 19X2	40	
Purchases	300	
	340	
Less Stock at 31 December 19X2	50	290
		210
Manufacturing wages		75
Gross profit		135
Less **Expenses:**		
Selling expenses	25	
Distribution expenses	10	
Admin. and financial expenses	40	75
Net profit before tax		60

Balance sheet as at 31 December 19X2

	£000	£000
Share capital		500
Reserves		250
		750
10% debentures		150
Capital employed		900
Current liabilities:		
Overdraft	15	
Trade creditors (19X1 £35,000)	65	80
		980
Fixed assets		820
Current assets:		
Stock	50	
Debtors (19X1 £60,000)	110	
Bank	—	160
		980

You are now required to calculate the following:

1 The ordinary shareholders' interest.

2 The working capital.

3 The amount of debenture interest which would have been included in the admin. and financial expenses.

4 The gross profit/sales %.

5 The net profit/sales %.

6 The acid test.

7 Return on capital employed (return on assets).

8 Average collection period.

9 Average credit period taken.

10 The rate of stock turnover.

11 Sales to fixed assets.

12 The gearing (treating the bank overdraft as a current liability).

13 The interest cover.

14 Give two reasons why you cannot compute some of the investment ratios.

Having completed this assessment you can compare your answers with the suggested answers on pages 189–91.

SELF-ASSESSMENT

Woodcroft plc

You have been supplied with the following data relating to Woodcroft plc for the years 19X7 and 19X8:

	19X7 £000	19X8 £000
Sales	1,200	1,600
Net profit before tax	120	180
Net profit after tax	80	130
Ordinary dividends (paid and proposed)	60	70

Balance sheet

	£000	19X7 £000	£000	19X8 £000
Capital employed:				
Ordinary shares (£1 each)		100		100
Reserves		100		160
		200		260
Employment of capital:				
Fixed assets		100		120
Current assets (19X6)				
Stock (160)	200		180	
Debtors (260)	300		340	
	500		520	
Less **Current liabilities** (19X6)				
Creditors (120)	160		180	
Proposed dividend	40		60	
Bank overdraft	200		140	
	400	100	380	140
		200		260

Calculate the following ratios for both 19X7 and 19X8, making brief comments about each of your answers:

Liquidity:
  Current ratio
  Acid test (quick ratio)
Profitability:
  Net profit to sales
  Return on investment (return on assets)
Efficiency:
  Average collection period
  Credit period taken
  Stock turnover
Investment:
  Earnings/shareholders' equity
  Dividend cover
  Earnings per ordinary share (EPS)

When you have completed this exercise, please check your answers with the suggested answers on pages 191–3.

SELF-ASSESSMENT

Nether Ltd and Thong Ltd

You are provided with the following accounting information for Nether Ltd and Thong Ltd for the year 19X8:

	Nether Ltd £000		Thong Ltd £000
Sales	125		250
Net profit before tax	25		40
Net profit after tax	20		32
Share capital (£1 shares)	100		100
Reserves	20		50
	£120		£150
Fixed assets	100		120

Current assets:				
Stock	25		60	
Debtors	20		30	
Cash	15		—	
	60		90	

Current liabilities:				
Creditors	40		35	
Bank overdraft	—		25	
	40	20	60	30
Net assets		£120		£150

Calculate the following ratios for 19X8 for both Nether Ltd and Thong Ltd in order to compare the performances of both companies (the industry average for each ratio is given in parentheses following the ratio):

Liquidity:
   Current ratio (2.00)
   Acid test (quick ratio) (0.90)
Profitability:
   Net profit before tax to sales (20%)
   Return on investment (return on assets) (24%)

Efficiency:
   Average collection period (60 days)
   Credit period taken (70 days)
   Stock turnover (7 times)
Investment:
   Earnings/shareholders' equity (20%)
   Earnings per ordinary share (£0.30)

Having made your calculations and comparisons, prepare a brief draft of your conclusions and recommendations.

When you have completed this self-assessment, please check your answers with the suggested answers on pages 193–5.

The limitations of ratio analysis

One of the principal limitations of ratio analysis is the inadequacy of the source data (i.e. trading accounts, profit and loss accounts and balance sheets) which may be caused by the following:

☐ The way in which the accounting concepts are applied, for instance the use of subjective judgement, and the inconsistency with which certain figures are calculated.

☐ Preparing accounts with the tax authorities in mind, e.g. the distinction between repairs and renewals and fixed assets is open to differing interpretations.

☐ A change in the accounting policies.

☐ Off-balance-sheet financing, e.g. the renting or leasing of machinery and plant.

☐ Window dressing, i.e. making the accounts look better or worse than they really are, e.g. having a special effort to collect cash in from debtors in the last few months of the accounting period. This means that the debtors' figure at the year end could be totally unrepresentative of the position that existed throughout the period.

This means that interfirm comparisons can be extremely difficult because the firms concerned could be using different accounting policies, applying the concepts in different ways and could be affected by off-balance-sheet financing, etc. This is why the most accurate and realistic comparisons are those which look at a company over a number of years. Even then, adjustments may have to be made, to allow for changes in accounting policies, inflation, etc.

Another major limitation arises from the way in which some of the ratios are computed, for example the following:

☐ The treatment of the bank overdraft. Is it really a current liability? Nowadays, many companies do use it as a long-term source of funds. The way in which it is treated affects liquidity ratios and gearing ratios.

☐ Certain ratios use the sales figures when the cost of sales or the purchases figure (materials consumed) is more appropriate.

☐ Which profit figure should be used? Should it be:
(a) net profit before tax?
(b) net profit after tax?
(c) net profit before interest and tax (NPBIT)?

☐ The average creditors, debtors and stocks are calculated using opening and closing balances. What happens throughout the period would thus appear to be irrelevant. For an external analysis the information is simply not available, but for internal analysis purposes it should be.

Finally, the terminology used also acts as a limitation in that it does tend to confuse the user, for example capital employed, net assets and net worth can mean the same thing. Some gearing ratios include the bank overdraft, others exclude it. Return on investment can be called return on assets or return on capital employed, and so on.

SELF-ASSESSMENT

The problems of interfirm comparison

Study the data given in Figure 9.23 for some companies in the textile industry. Listed below are two possible reasons why a comparison of the financial performance of the textile companies is difficult:

1 Some of them may be highly diversified and others may not be.

2 Their product ranges could be significantly different.

See if you can think of four more reasons why it is difficult to make comparisons.

When you have completed this self-assessment, please check your answers with the suggested answers on page 195.

Industry			Performance		
Textiles	Year end	Turnover £m	Return on investment %	Net profit/ sales %	Stock turnover
Company					
A	Sept X2	30.7	24.5	9.7	3.7
B	Dec X2	24.1	20.7	11.3	2.7
C	Mar X3	82.6	41.3	18.8	3.6
D	Mar X3	15.6	13.8	8.0	3.1
E	Jun X3	23.9	32.2	13.1	10.3
F	Mar X3	10.7	14.4	7.2	2.6
G	Mar X3	119.7	15.1	6.1	3.2
H	Dec X2	7.5	15.8	7.4	4.1
I	Sept X2	7.6	31.1	13.3	16.0
J	Feb X3	29.2	22.4	9.4	3.5
K	Mar X3	76.4	22.2	10.7	3.6
L	Apr X3	10.2	30.1	13.3	3.1

Figure 9.23 Industry figures – textiles.

Accounting ratios: The essence

Ratio analysis

Ratio analysis is a tool which is used in order to compare and evaluate financial performance. The source data from which the ratios are calculated may be internal, e.g. the company's own trading and profit and loss account, appropriation account, balance sheet and data relating to debtors, creditors and stocks, etc.; or external in the form of the published accounts of other companies and industry figures which are available from a variety of sources.

Ratios can help to do the following:

☐ Indicate areas in which further investigation is needed.
☐ Highlight strengths and weaknesses.
☐ Provoke questions.

Ratios are of little value if they are used in isolation. To be useful, they need to be viewed in conjunction with other data, such as the following:

☐ Information about the management.
☐ Industry figures, which provide a yardstick with which realistic comparisons can be made.

- ☐ The value of fixed assets and investments.
- ☐ Opportunity costs, e.g. the returns available from alternative investments.
- ☐ Government regulations/legislation already passed or pending.
- ☐ Security, i.e. the degree to which the company has used its assets as security for loans and debentures.

The ratios

The following ratios should help you to make a reasonable assessment of the financial performance of a company.

Profitability
The gross profit to sales ratio is expressed as follows:

$$\frac{\text{Gross profit}}{\text{Sales}} \times 100$$

It indicates the average gross margin (mark-up) which is being made on the products/services which are being sold.

The net profit to sales (net margin) ratio is expressed as follows:

$$\frac{\text{Net profit before tax}}{\text{Sales}} \times 100$$

This shows how much profit is being generated by the sales and in addition to the effects of the gross profit it provides an indication as to what is happening to the overheads.

The return on investment (ROI) ratio (also called return on capital employed (ROCE) and return on assets) is expressed as follows:

$$\frac{\text{Net profit before interest and tax (NPBIT)}}{\text{Capital employed (less intangibles, if any)}} \times 100$$

This gives the overall return on all of the capital which has been invested in the business, i.e. a measure of the productivity of all the capital invested in the business irrespective of its source.

Liquidity ratios
The current ratio (or the ratio of current assets to current liabilities) is expressed as follows:

$$\frac{\text{Current assets}}{\text{Current liabilities}}$$

This provides an indication of whether the company has excess liquidity, satisfactory liquidity or liquidity problems. It provides an indication of the company's ability to pay its short-term debts.

The acid test (or quick) ratio is expressed as follows:

$$\frac{\text{Liquid assets (i.e. current assets less stocks)}}{\text{Current liabilities}}$$

This is a key ratio used in the management of working capital, which looks at the ability to pay short-term debts with the liquid assets. As a general rule, this ratio is expected to be around one to one, i.e. £1 of liquid assets to every £1 owing to current liabilities. However, in practice the liquid assets tend to be less than £1 for every £1 owing to current liabilities.

Efficiency ratios
These ratios look at asset utilization and provide an insight into the efficiency of inventory (stock) control and credit control.

The average collection period ratio is expressed as follows:

$$\frac{\text{Average debtors}}{\text{Sales}} \times 365$$

This provides us with an indication of how long it is taking us to collect the amounts owing from our credit customers, i.e. our debtors.

The credit period taken ratio is expressed as follows:

$$\frac{\text{Average creditors}}{\text{Purchases (or sales if the purchases figure is not available)}} \times 365$$

This tells us the average time it takes us to pay our suppliers of goods on credit. Note that creditors do represent a source of short-term financing to the company.

The stock turnover ratio is expressed as follows:

$$\frac{\text{Cost of sales (or sales)}}{\text{Average stock (i.e. opening plus closing stock divided by two)}}$$

= The rate of turnover

This shows the number of times which the average stock held is sold in a given period of time.

The sales to fixed assets ratio is expressed as follows:

1. $\dfrac{\text{Sales}}{\text{Fixed assets}} = $ The overall efficiency with which the fixed assets are used

2.

$$\frac{\text{Sales}}{\text{Manufacturing fixed assets}} = \text{A measure of the utilization of manufacturing fixed assets}$$

Capital structure ratios

The gearing (or leverage) ratio is expressed as follows:

$$\frac{\text{Debt, i.e. other forms of long-term financing (with or without the bank overdraft, as appropriate)}}{\text{Debt (with or without the bank overdraft) + ordinary share capital + reserves}} \times 100$$

This looks at the proportion of other forms of long-term financing in relation to the total long-term financing and is of particular significance to financial management and the providers of finance.

The debt/equity ratio is expressed as follows:

$$\frac{\text{Debt}}{\text{Equity}}$$

Those companies with a high proportion of debt to equity, i.e. those which are highly geared, tend to be at greater risk in periods where trading conditions are poor. This is because they have to pay interest or repay capital and interest on debentures/loans irrespective of whether they are performing well or badly.

Many companies nowadays do use their bank overdraft as a long-term source of funds. Note that there are many more gearing ratios and that some authors exclude the preference shares from the other forms of long-term financing and treat it in the same way as the equity.

The interest cover ratio is expressed as follows:

$$\frac{\text{Net profit before interest and tax}}{\text{Loan and debenture interest}}$$

This ratio shows how well the company can cover the interest that it has to pay out. It is expressed as the number of times that it can cover the interest payments. If the preference dividend is added to the loan and debenture interest the ratio then becomes the fixed charge cover.

Employee ratios

Employee ratios assess the productivity of labour in terms of sales and net profit. The ones which were covered earlier in this chapter were:

☐ Average remuneration per employee.

□ Net profit per employee.

□ Sales per employee.

□ Directors' efficiency.

Investment ratios

Investment ratios are of particular significance to directors, shareholders, analysts, would-be investors and competitors.

The earnings/shareholders' equity (return on equity) ratio is expressed as follows:

$$\frac{\text{Net profit after tax, less preference dividends (if any)}}{\text{Equity (i.e. issued ordinary share capital + reserves)}} \times 100$$

This ratio provides the ordinary shareholders with an idea of what their return on investment is. The profit figure which is used in the calculation represents what is left for them after paying everything else including interest and tax, and dividends on preference shares.

The dividend yield ratio can be expressed as follows:

$$\frac{\text{Dividend per ordinary share}}{\text{Market price per ordinary share}} \times 100$$

This ratio relates the profit distributed as dividend to the share price. It does not measure the return on investment for a shareholder because there are also the capital gains on their shares to consider. However, it does provide a potential investor with an indication of the expected rate of return on investment in terms of cash paid out.

The earnings per ordinary share or earnings per share (EPS) ratio is expressed as follows:

$$\frac{\text{Net profit after tax less preference dividend}}{\text{Number of ordinary shares issued}}$$

This represents the earning power per share.

The dividend cover (on ordinary shares) ratio is expressed as follows:

$$\frac{\text{Earnings per share}}{\text{Dividend per share}}$$

This ratio shows how many times the company can cover its ordinary share dividends from its current earnings. It can also be calculated in the following way:

$$\frac{\text{Net profit after tax less preference dividend}}{\text{Total ordinary share dividend}}$$

The price earnings (PE) ratio is expressed as follows:

$$\frac{\text{Market price per ordinary share}}{\text{Earnings per ordinary share}}$$

This ratio expresses the relationship between the company's ability to generate profits and the market price of its ordinary shares.

The capitalization rate (or earnings yield) ratio is the PE ratio turned upside down, and is expresed as follows:

$$\frac{\text{Earnings per ordinary share}}{\text{Market price per ordinary share}} \times 100$$

It provides shareholders and investors with an indication of the current performance of the ordinary shares, i.e. it provides a measure of the cost of the equity share capital.

Value added statements and ratios
Value added statements show how the value added (the wealth created), i.e. sales less materials and services bought from outside suppliers, is distributed between the stakeholders. The stakeholders of a company are the employees, the providers of capital, the government, and the company itself by means of depreciation and retained earnings.

Ratios can be computed using value added to measure the productivity of labour, capital and fixed assets and also the growth of the original inputs.

Using the information

Information can be used in the following ways:

☐ When you look at comparative figures. For example, this year compared to last year, or company A compared to company B. It is useful to make working notes on each ratio/group of ratios to explain the variances and to highlight strengths and weaknesses, etc.

☐ If a ratio analysis is to be useful, it needs to be based on several years' figures so that trends can be identified and emerging problems detected.

☐ The quest for a 'yardstick', i.e. something against which performance can be measured, can be partly solved by using industry figures.

Limitations
Ratio analysis does have limitations, the principal ones being:

☐ The inadequacy of the source data, i.e. the final accounts, for example concerning the application of concepts and accounting policies, 'off-balance-sheet financing' and 'window dressing', etc.

☐ The way in which the ratios are computed, for example the treatment of the bank overdraft as a long- or short-term source of finance; using the sales figure when purchases or cost of sales figures would be more appropriate; the profit figure could be one of many, for example, net profit before tax, net profit after tax, etc.; the way in which the average debtors, creditors and stock are arrived at, i.e. taking no account of what happens during the intervening period.

☐ The terminology can be very confusing.

Interfirm comparison
If you have to carry out an interfirm comparison, beware! You cannot just compare with another firm in the same industrial sector. You also need to try to select companies which are in the same industrial sector and which also have some of the following characteristics:

☐ Have a similar product range.

☐ Are of a similar size.

☐ Have the same year end.

☐ Use similar accounting policies.

☐ Finance their assets in a similar manner, i.e. the extent to which they use 'off-balance-sheet financing'.

☐ Have revalued their buildings around the same date.

☐ Employ the same kind of production methods.

☐ Are located in an area where overhead costs are similar.

☐ Arrive at the year-end stock valuations using similar methods/practices.

Further reading

Berry, A. and Jarvis, R., *Accounting in a Business Context* (Chapman and Hall, 1994).

Bird, P. (ed. B. Rutherford), *Understanding Company Accounts*, 3rd edition (Pitman, 1989).

Edwards, J. R. and Mellett, H. J., *Introduction to Accounting* (Paul Chapman Publishing, 1995).

McKenzie, W., *The Financial Times Guide To: Using and Interpreting Company Accounts* (Pitman, 1994).

Parker, R. H., *Understanding Company Financial Statements* (Penguin, 1988).

Sneyd, P., *Principles of Accounting and Finance* (Routledge, 1994).

Sources of industry data

- [] *U.K. Industrial Performance Analysis* (published annually, ICC Business Publications Ltd).
- [] Extel Cards.
- [] The Company Reports Section of a library, e.g. covering *The Times'* 1,000 companies.
- [] On the computer *Micro View* by Extel as used by leading business schools, and *Micro Extat* as used by leading business schools.
- [] *Financial Analysis Made Easy* (CD Rom Publishing Co, 1995).

10

The published accounts of companies

Objectives

It is not the objective of this chapter that you become expert in preparing published accounts. (For the rest of this chapter we will, in the main, use the description published accounts to mean the annual report and accounts of a company.) The objective of this chapter is, that by having some hands-on experience with a series of projects you will be able to add to your existing knowledge, and by looking at some published accounts be able to do the following:

□ Understand the accounts.

□ Use the accounts.

□ Analyze the accounts by using some of the ratios described in Chapter 9.

□ Seek explanations about items which are new to you, such as extraordinary items, from tutors/accountants/business contacts, etc.

□ Appreciate how certain of the figures have been calculated, such as fixed assets.

□ Know the kind of information which goes into the directors' report.

□ Identify differences in the accounting policies which are being followed by a number of companies.

□ Look at how a profit and loss account or a balance sheet item is made up by a study of the appropriate note.

□ Review the statistical data/ratio analysis which is included.

□ See which of the statutory formats for the profit and loss account and the balance sheet have been adopted.

☐ Understand the cash flow statement.

This chapter also provides you with a brief introduction to the role of the auditor.

The published accounts

For external reporting purposes, UK companies are bound by law to produce a set of accounts for publication, i.e. their annual report and accounts.

The Companies Act 1985/89 prescribes the following:

☐ The format of the published accounts.

☐ The contents of the published accounts.

☐ The rules for computing figures which appear in those accounts.

Companies must now do the following:

☐ Prepare their published profit and loss account according to any one of the four statutory formats (see Figure 10.1).

☐ Publish a balance sheet using one of the two statutory formats (see Figure 10.2).

☐ Adopt historical accounting rules which with one or two exceptions tend to follow existing practice. However, they may adopt any of the alternative accounting rules which are permitted by the Companies Act.

The profit and loss account formats

Must be prepared on either:

- An operational analysis basis
  (formats 1 and 2)

     or

- A basis which analyzes costs by
  type of expense (formats 3 and 4).

The basis adopted must be applied consistently from year to year, any change or reasons for the change must be dislosed by way of a note.

You will find these formats on pages 158–64.

Figure 10.1 Published profit and loss accounts.

The balance sheet formats

The balance sheet may be prepared either:

- In vertical format (format 1)

or

- Using an assets.liabilities basis (format 2).

You will find these formats on pages 160–2.

Figure 10.2 Published balance sheets.

The directors' report must disclose:

Information about the business development of the company and its subsidiaries as follows:

- A fair review during and at the end of the financial year, for example of turnover, profits, taxation, trading conditions, markets.
- Important events which have occurred since the year end, such as trading conditions, acquisitions, competition.
- Likely future developments.
- Research and development activities.

Particulars of the acquisition and disposal of its own shares, by any company (private or public).

Figure 10.3 The directors' report.

- Provide information in the directors' report as indicated in Figure 10.3.
- Include certain specific information in the notes to the accounts, such as the source of any increase or decrease in fixed assets.
- Ignore certain provisions contained in the Companies Act if doing so means that the accounts will show a true and fair view.
- Publish a section dealing with accounting policies.

Reporting exemptions for small and medium-sized companies

The Companies Act provides that small and medium-sized companies are exempt from filing certain documents and information with the Registrar of Companies (see Figure 10.4).

**The Companies Act's definition of small
and medium-sized companies**

Does not include:

- Public limited companies.
- Banking, insurance and shipping companies.
- Groups containing the above-mentioned types of companies.

Must satisfy any two of the following three conditions taken from the 1989
Companies Act for the current or previous year:

	Small company	Medium company
Turnover should not exceed	£2 m	£8 m
Total assets at the year end must not exceed	£0.975 m	£3.9 m
Average number of employees (calculated on a weekly basis) should not exceed	50	250

These limits are revised from time to time.

Figure 10.4 The Companies Act's definition of small and medium-sized companies.

Filing exemptions for small companies

Small companies may file a *modified balance sheet* but need not file:

☐ A profit and loss account.
☐ The directors' report.
☐ Details of higher-paid employees' and directors' emoluments.
☐ Certain notes, e.g. accounting policies, etc.

Filing exemptions for medium-sized companies

Medium-sized companies may file a modified profit and loss account but
do not have to disclose certain items by way of note.

Auditors and the modified accounts

A special auditors' report must verify that all the exemption criteria have
been met. In addition the full text of the auditors' report contained in the
full accounts must be filed with the modified accounts.

The statutory formats

The Companies Act 1985/89 provides formats which must be used in the published accounts of companies. However, there is a choice, for instance four profit and loss formats and two balance sheet formats.

The statutory formats were introduced by the Companies Act 1981 and are as follows.

Profit and loss account formats

Format 1 (operational basis)
1. Turnover
2. Cost of sales
3. Gross profit or loss
4. Distribution costs
5. Administrative expenses
6. Other operating income
7. Income from shares in group companies
8. Income from shares in related companies
9. Income from other fixed asset investments
10. Other interest receivable and similar income
11. Amounts written off investments
12. Interest payable and similar charges
13. Tax on profit or loss on ordinary activities
14. Profit or loss on ordinary activities after taxation
15. Extraordinary income
16. Extraordinary charges
17. Extraordinary profit or loss
18. Tax on ordinary profit or loss
19. Other taxes not shown under the above items
20. Profit or loss for the financial year

Format 2 (operational basis)
1. Turnover
2. Change in stocks of finished goods and work-in-progress
3. Own work capitalized
4. Other operating income
5. (a) Raw materials and consumables
   (b) Other external charges
6. Staff costs:
   (a) Wages and salaries
   (b) Social security costs
   (c) Other pension costs

7. Depreciation and other amounts written off tangible and intangible fixed assets
8. Other operating charges
9. Income from shares in group companies
10. Income from shares in related companies
11. Income from other fixed asset investments
12. Other interest receivable and similar income
13. Amounts written off investments
14. Interest payable and similar charges
15. Tax on profit or loss on ordinary activities
16. Profit or loss on ordinary activities after taxation
17. Extraordinary income
18. Extraordinary charges
19. Extraordinary profit or loss
20. Tax on ordinary profit or loss
21. Other taxes not shown under the above items
22. Profit or loss for the financial year

Format 3 (type of expense basis)

A. Charges
1. Cost of sales
2. Distribution costs
3. Administrative expenses
4. Amounts written off investments
5. Interest payable and similar charges
6. Tax on profit or loss on ordinary activities
7. Profit or loss on ordinary activities after taxation
8. Extraordinary charges
9. Tax on extraordinary profit or loss
10. Other taxes not shown under the above items
11. Profit or loss for the financial year

B. Income
1. Turnover
2. Other operating income
3. Income from shares in group companies
4. Income from shares in related companies
5. Income from other fixed asset investments
6. Other interest receivable and similar income
7. Profit or loss on ordinary activities after taxation
8. Extraordinary income
9. Profit or loss for the financial year

Format 4 (type of expense basis)

A. Charges

1. Reduction in stocks of finished goods and in work-in-progress
2. (a) Raw materials and consumables
   (b) Other external charges
3. Staff costs:
   (a) Wages and salaries
   (b) Social security costs
   (c) Other pension costs
4. (a) Depreciation and other amounts written off tangible and intangible fixed assets
   (b) Exceptional amounts written off current assets
5. Other operating charges
6. Amounts written off investments
7. Interest payable and similar charges
8. Tax on profit or loss on ordinary activities after taxation
9. Profit or loss on ordinary activities
10. Extraordinary charges
11. Tax on extraordinary profit or loss
12. Other taxes not shown under the above items
13. Profit or loss for the financial year

B. Income

1. Turnover
2. Increase in stocks of finished goods and in work-in-progress
3. Own work capitalized
4. Other operating income
5. Income from shares in group companies
6. Income from shares in related companies
7. Income from other fixed asset investments
8. Other interest receivable and similar income
9. Profit or loss on ordinary activities after taxation
10. Extraordinary income
11. Profit or loss for the financial year

Balance sheet formats

Format 1

A. Called up share capital not paid

B. Fixed assets

   I Intangible assets

      1. Development costs

    2. Concessions, patents, licences, trade marks and similar rights and assets

    3. Goodwill

    4. Payments on account

II Tangible assets

    1. Land and buildings

    2. Plant and machinery

    3. Fixtures, fittings, tools and equipment

    4. Payments on account and assets in course of construction

III Investments

    1. Shares in group companies

    2. Loans to group companies

    3. Shares in related companies

    4. Loans to related companies

    5. Other investments other than loans

    6. Other loans

    7. Own shares

C. Current assets

  I Stocks

    1. Raw materials and consumables

    2. Work-in-progress

    3. Finished goods and goods for resale

    4. Payments on account

  II Debtors

    1. Trade debtors

    2. Amounts owed by group companies

    3. Amounts owed by related companies

    4. Other debtors

    5. Called up share capital not paid

    6. Prepayments and accrued income

  III Investments

    1. Shares in group companies

    2. Own shares

    3. Other investments

  IV Cash at bank in hand

D. Prepayments and accrued income

E. Creditors: amounts falling due within one year

    1. Debenture loans

    2. Bank loans and overdrafts

    3. Payments received on account

    4. Trade creditors

    5. Bills of exchange payable

    6. Amounts owed to group companies

     7. Amounts owed to related companies
     8. Other creditors including taxation and social security
     9. Accruals and deferred income

F. Net current assets (liabilities)

G. Total assets less current liabilities

H. Creditors: amounts falling due after more than one year
     1. Debenture loans
     2. Bank loans and overdrafts
     3. Payments received on account
     4. Trade creditors
     5. Bills of exchange payable
     6. Amounts owed to group companies
     7. Amounts owed to related companies
     8. Other creditors including taxation and social security
     9. Accruals and deferred income

I. Provisions for liabilities and charges
     1. Pensions and similar obligations
     2. Taxation, including deferred taxation
     3. Other provisions

J. Accruals and deferred income

K. Capital and reserves
     I Called up share capital
     II Share premium account
     III Revaluation reserve
     IV Other reserves
       1. Capital redemption reserve
       2. Reserve for own shares
       3. Reserves provided for by articles of association
       4. Other reserves
     V Profit and loss account

Format 2

Assets

A. Called up share capital not paid

B. Fixed assets
     I Intangible assets
       1. Development costs
       2. Concessions, patents, licences, trade marks and similar rights
          and assets
       3. Goodwill
       4. Payments on account

    II Tangible assets
1. Land and buildings
2. Plant and machinery
3. Fixtures, fittings, tools and equipment
4. Payments on account and assets in course of construction

   III Investments
1. Shares in group companies
2. Loans to group companies
3. Shares in related companies
4. Loans to related companies
5. Other investments other than loans
6. Other loans
7. Own shares

C. Current assets

    I Stocks
1. Raw materials and consumables
2. Work-in-progress
3. Finished goods and goods for resale
4. Payments on account

   II Debtors
1. Trade debtors
2. Amounts owed by group companies
3. Amounts owed by related companies
4. Other debtors
5. Called up share capital not paid
6. Prepayments and accrued income

   III Investments
1. Shares in group companies
2. Own shares
3. Other investments

   IV Cash at bank and in hand

D. Prepayments and accrued income

Liabilities

A. Capital and reserves

    I Called up share capital

   II Share premium

   III Revaluation reserve

   IV Other reserves
1. Capital redemption reserve
2. Reserve for own shares
3. Reserves provided for by articles of association
4. Other reserves

    V Profit and loss account

B. Provisions for liabilities and charges
    1. Pensions and similar obligations
    2. Taxation including deferred taxation
    3. Other provisions

C. Creditors
    1. Debenture loans
    2. Bank loans and overdrafts
    3. Payments received on account
    4. Trade creditors
    5. Bills of exchange payable
    6. Amounts owed to group companies
    7. Amounts owed to related companies
    8. Other creditors including taxation and social security
    9. Accruals and deferred income

D. Accruals and deferred income

Groups' (consolidated) accounts

Where another company, i.e. a holding company, owns/controls another company/other companies, i.e. subsidiary companies, group accounts are published. These will include a consolidated profit and loss account, and a consolidated balance sheet. A study of group accounts is outside the scope of this book. Suffice it to say that they do exist and you will, no doubt, come into contact with them.

What kind of information must a company publish in its accounts/notes to the accounts?

The short answer to this question is enough to fill a book, i.e. a lot! The following is a brief summary of some of the items which you are likely to encounter:

☐ A breakdown of how the operating profit and turnover figures have been arrived at.

☐ Details of loans and an analysis of interest payments, e.g. on bank overdraft and loans.

☐ Taxation details.

☐ Extraordinary items, e.g. the profit or loss on the sale of long-term investments.

☐ Dividends paid and proposed.

☐ Details of the remuneration paid/pension contributions relating to employees and directors.

☐ Retained earnings and movements in reserves.

☐ If significant, charges for the rent or hire of equipment, plant and machinery, and vehicles, etc.

☐ Auditors' remuneration.

☐ Details of investments/investment income and rental income.

☐ Details of movements in fixed assets and the depreciation of fixed assets, e.g. acquisitions, disposals, revaluations, etc.

☐ Capital commitments.

☐ How the individual current asset/current liability figures were arrived at, e.g. stocks, debtors, bank, cash, creditors, etc.

☐ An analysis of share capital, share premium, reserves and the profit and loss account showing the source of any increase or decrease.

☐ Information about pensions.

☐ Details of any contingent liability, e.g. a debt which the company may or may not be called upon to pay under a warranty.

☐ Post-balance-sheet events, e.g. the acquisition of a significant holding of ordinary shares in another company.

☐ Changes to accounting policies.

☐ Corresponding figures for the previous accounting period.

An introduction to the role of the auditor

The role of the auditor has been described as being that of a watchdog, rather than a bloodhound. The objectives of an audit are the following:

☐ To verify and report upon the financial state of an organization, i.e. a true and fair view.

☐ To detect errors and fraud.

☐ To prevent errors and fraud.

There are various classes of audit, as follows:

☐ Statutory, for example for limited companies, building societies, etc.

☐ Private firms, by Letters of Appointment.

☐ Trust accounts.

☐ Partnerships (Partnership Agreement).

☐ Internal audit by employees of the company/organization.

A knowledge of basic documents is very important for conducting an audit – these basic documents include invoices, statements, credit notes, goods received notes, etc.

An outline of the work of an auditor can be summarized by the words verify, examine, report, enquire and check (VEREC). VEREC can be expanded upon as follows:

☐ *Verify*
The existence, ownership and basis of valuation of the assets and ensure that the liabilities are fully and accurately disclosed.

☐ *Examine* (vouch)
Vouchers and any other evidence that may be required to prove that the entries in the books of account are complete and authentic.

☐ *Report*
To the owners whether the balance sheet shows a true and fair view of the affairs, and the profit and loss account a true and fair view of the profit or loss for the financial period under review.

☐ *Enquire*
As to the authority for transactions and see that all benefits which should have been accounted for have in fact been received.

☐ *Check*
The arithmetic, i.e. the accuracy of the books of account.

Published accounts projects

As indicated in the objectives at the beginning of this chapter, you are expected to learn a lot about published accounts through some hands-on practical experience.

A lot of what you encounter will be familiar to you. You will come across many of the terms which have been used throughout this text. However, the format in which the information is presented is quite different. The profit and loss account and the balance sheet tend to include the totals of principal items or groups of items, and these are then explained through a series of quite detailed notes (notes to the accounts) which are designed to show the workings and any further information required by the Companies Act. The published accounts will also include the following:

□ An auditors' report.
□ A statement of accounting policies.
□ A directors' report.
□ A cash flow statement.
□ A statistical analysis.

Before you start the projects, you will need to acquire, through friends or by writing to the companies concerned, the following items:

□ A copy of the published accounts of three different companies which are in the same industrial sector.
□ A copy of the published accounts of two other companies which are in different industrial sectors from the above and from each other.

If you work for a public limited company, i.e. a plc, this could provide you with a starting-point for one set of published accounts.

PROJECT 1 *Terms*

Select one set of published accounts. Then look through the profit and loss account, balance sheet and notes to the accounts, and list all of the terms which you have not come across before.

Find out what these terms mean by using other books such as the Collins *Dictionary of Business* (1995), tutors, friends, accountants, etc.

PROJECT 2 *Accounting policies*

Take the published accounts of the three companies from the same industrial sector. Compare their accounting policies and highlight the principal differences using a columnar analysis drafted along the lines shown in Figure 10.5.

Accounting policy	Company A	Company B	Company C
Depreciation Plant and machinery			

Figure 10.5 Form to compare companies' accounting policies.

PROJECT 3 *Accounting policies*

Now, take the published accounts from the two other companies and see how their accounting policies compare with those which you analyzed in Project 2.

Remember, the accounting policies which are adopted do affect the reported profits or losses!

PROJECT 4 *Directors' reports*

Take three sets of published accounts from three different industrial sectors and read their directors' reports.

See if you can identify what they have in common and if they match up to the contents listed in Figure 10.3.

PROJECT 5 *Balance sheet workings*

Take any one set of published accounts. Find the following items in the balance sheet:

☐ fixed assets;

☐ investments (if any);

☐ share capital;

☐ reserves (including the profit and loss account).

Then find the appropriate note which illustrates how these figures have been arrived at, and see if you can follow the workings.

PROJECT 6 *Profit and loss account workings*

Take any set of published accounts and study the profit and loss account together with the appropriate notes to see how the following figures are arrived at:

☐ turnover;

☐ interest;

☐ profit on ordinary activities before taxation;

☐ extraordinary items (if any);

☐ dividends.

PROJECT 7 *Cash flow statement*

Having studied funds flow analysis earlier in this text, look at one or two of the companies' published cash flow statements, and see if you can understand them.

PROJECT 8 *Accounting ratios*

Using the published accounts from the three companies from the same industrial sector, critically examine the ratios which are used to analyze their financial performance. Also, see if you can calculate some of them.

There are many more projects which could be carried out using published accounts, such as a long-term company financial history or a five-year analysis/critical evaluation.

The published accounts of companies: The essence

The Companies Act 1985/89 requires companies to publish their accounts, i.e. their annual report and accounts. The published accounts/reports should do the following:

☐ Contain a profit and loss account and balance sheet in one of the prescribed formats. A selection has to be made from four profit and loss formats and two balance sheet formats, see pages 158–64.
☐ Contain figures which have been computed according to the rules laid down by the Companies Act.
☐ Contain the information required by the Companies Act.

The published accounts will tend to include the following items:

☐ Information about directors.
☐ The directors' report, see page 156.
☐ An auditors' report.
☐ Profit and loss account.
☐ Balance sheet.
☐ A cash flow statement (i.e. a funds flow).
☐ Statement of accounting policies.
☐ Notes to the accounts.
☐ Statistical information, e.g. financial ratios, etc.

The published profit and loss account and the balance sheet are in effect summaries of the detailed information which appears in the notes to the accounts.

Companies do have to file a copy of their published accounts with the Registrar of Companies. However, small and medium-sized companies are exempt from certain provisions, see page 157.

Who needs the published accounts? There are many parties interested in the published accounts of companies, for example directors, shareholders, bankers, creditors, investors, employees, analysts, etc.

What can we find out about a company from its published accounts? The published accounts contain a wealth of information about the company, for example, information about the following:

□ Important events, future projects, and research and development activities.

□ Directors and employees.

□ How the operating profit has been arrived at.

□ Taxation.

□ Extraordinary items.

□ Dividends.

□ Retained earnings, reserves and share capital.

□ Rent or hire of equipment, plant, machinery and vehicles.

□ Auditors' remuneration.

□ Investment and rental income.

□ How the fixed assets, depreciation, current assets and current liabilities figures were computed.

□ Capital commitments.

□ Contingent liabilities.

□ Statistical information and corresponding figures.

The role of the auditor can be summed up by the term VEREC, i.e. verify, examine, report, enquire and check.

You can learn a lot about published accounts by reviewing a selection of them. This review, when combined with your knowledge gained from the earlier chapters of this text, should enable you to find out information about a wide variety of matters. You will, of course, have lots of questions which you would like answers to. You may find the answers to some of these questions from other books, tutors, friends and accountants, etc. It is this investigative process, i.e. the needs of an enquiring mind, that will help you to find out more and more about the published accounts of companies.

'What I do, I know.' Hence, the projects which were included earlier on pages 167–8.

Further reading

Berry, A. and Jarvis, R., *Accounting in a Business Context* (Chapman and Hall, 1994).

Bird, P. (ed. Rutherford, B.), *Understanding Company Accounts*, 3rd edition (Pitman, 1989).

Glantier, M. W. E. and Underdown, B., *Accounting Theory and Practice* (Pitman, 1994).

Oldcorn, R., *Company Accounts* (Macmillan, 1989).

Parker, R. H., *Understanding Company Financial Statements* (Penguin, 1988).

Suggested answers to self-assessment problems

Accounting concepts (Chapter 2)

Answer	Comments
1. Inflation.	Monetary values are not always a stable measure.
2. (c)	A transaction will be included in the sales figure when it has been invoiced. The invoice generates the data which are needed by the recording system.

3.	£000	Note that if you include the
Cash sales	11	£5,000 cash from August credit
Credit sales	29	sales in your calculation, you
	—	would be including that
August sales	£40	amount twice. It is already
	—	included in the £29,000, the £29,000 being all the credit sales for August.

4. My company would lose money because of the time lag between paying the tax on the sale and	This is an example of an 'opportunity cost', i.e. the alternative which has been

receiving the tax relief. The money lost represents the interest which could have been earned on the money which was used to pay the tax.

forgone. If the tax on this sale did not have to be paid, the money would have been available for other uses, e.g. investing in a bank deposit account.

---

5. They use the cut-off procedure to ensure that those items of stock which arrive just before the year end are either included or excluded from their closing stock valuation.

Those goods which arrive after the cut-off date are excluded from stock and should, therefore, also be excluded from the purchases figure. The system also applies to sales.

---

6. Conservatism or prudence.

This explains why accountants tend to have a cautious image.

---

7. Materiality.

However, what is significant will depend upon the judgement of the decision maker and the size of the company/organization.

---

8. Business rent for the year to 30 June 19X3:

You could reconcile this by saying that the year is made up of:

	£000		£000
Prepaid rent 1 July 19X2 to 30 September 19X2	15	9 months to 31 March 19X3	45
Add Amount paid to 31 March 19X3	30	plus 3 months of the year to 31 March 19X4	18
Amount paid to 31 March 19X4	72		—
	—		£63
	117		—
Less Amount prepaid 1 July 19X3 to 31 March 19X4 (9 months) 9/12 × 72 c/f =	54		
	—		
	63		
	—		

i.e. the rates charge for the period 1 July 19X2 to 30 June 19X3. The £54,000 would be shown as a prepayment in the 30 June 19X3 balance sheet and carried forward to the next financial year.

---

9. £12,000

The charge for the period will be £12,000 irrespective of whether or not it has been paid, as per the matching concept. The £1,000 owing would show up in the balance sheet for the period as an accrual/current liability.

---

10. Consistency should ensure that the accounts are more comparable. In addition to this, consistency also promotes objectivity.

Control accounts (Chapter 3)

Purchase ledger control account

		£000
Balance of creditors at 1 January 19X5		78
Period 1 January 19X5 to 31 January 19X5		
Add Goods bought on credit		25
	£000	103
Less Cash paid to creditors	37	
Discount allowed by creditors	3	
Goods returned	4	44
Balance of creditors at 31 January 19X5	=	£59

The £59,000 should agree with the total of all the balances on the individual accounts contained in the purchases (bought) ledger.

This account could have been prepared in double-entry format. However, it is not part of the double-entry system – it simply uses the totals generated by the system to provide an arithmetic proof. This is why control accounts are also called total accounts.

The trading and profit and loss account (Chapter 4)

1. Accounting period.

2. Income and expenditure account.

3. The accounting concepts, accounting standards, and relevant legislation. There are other standards which have not yet been mentioned in this text, such as International Accounting Standards (IASs), Statements of Recommended Practice (SORPs), etc.

4. The correct answer is (a).

Directors' fees and debenture interest should have already been deducted in computing the net profit or loss. They are considered to be charges which should be dealt with in the profit and loss account. They are **not** considered to be appropriations.

5.

	£000	£000
Sales		150
Less **Cost of sales**		
Opening stock	12	
Add Purchases	100	
	112	
Less Closing stock	18	94
Gross profit		56

(The cost of sales is £94,000.)

6. A manufacturing account.

7.

	£000	£000
Gross profit		184
Less **Expenses:**		
Expenses	63	
Depreciation	18	
Loan interest	4	
Directors' fees	24	109
Net profit before tax		75

Tax and dividends paid (or proposed) are dealt with in the appropriation account.

8. Gross margin, or the margin, or the mark-up.

9.

	Appropriation account	£
Net profit (after deducting directors' fees and loan interest) before tax		114
Less Tax		32
Net profit after tax		82
Less Dividends paid and proposed (£8 + £10)		18
		64
Add Balance of retained earnings b/f		38
Retained earnings c/f		£102

The description 'net profit before tax' relates to the figure which remains after deducting all of the relevant expenses for the period, including the directors' fees and loan interest, i.e. before appropriations.

10. P&L account balance and ploughed back profits.
    You may come across other descriptions, such as undistributed profits or unappropriated profits.

The balance sheet 1 (Chapter 5)

1. (a) statement
   (b) capital = assets less liabilities
   (c) has come from
       has gone to
   (d) as at
       frozen

2. Any three limitations from the following:
   ☐ The snapshot, i.e. it only shows the position at a particular point in time.
   ☐ The cost concept. It shows many of the assets at their historic cost or cost less depreciation. These book values can be significantly different to their real values.
   ☐ The money measurement concept. Important factors which cannot be measured in monetary terms are not shown in a balance sheet, for example morale, industrial relations, etc.
   ☐ Window dressing may be responsible for the production of figures which are totally unrepresentative of the situation which existed throughout the year.

3. The £400,000 is simply the historic cost of the equipment less the depreciation. This value, i.e. the book value, may be way out of line with the amount which could be received if the equipment was sold.

4. The stock figure shown in the balance sheet could have been subjected to window dressing. It could have been allowed to run down to a level which is so low, that it is not a true representation of the position which existed throughout the accounting period.
   Note that the debtors and creditors could have also been subject to window dressing. Window dressing, by understating or overstating them (when compared with their levels throughout the accounting period), can significantly affect the picture portrayed by the accounts.

5. The two concepts mentioned in the chapter which affect the figures which are disclosed in a balance sheet, were:

(a) the money measurement concept;
(b) the cost concept.

The balance sheet 2 (Chapter 5)

1. Capital represents an amount owing to whosoever invested it in the business, e.g. the shareholders.

2. Ordinary share capital *plus* reserves *plus* long-term debt (long-term liabilities) equals the capital employed.

   Note that some writers also include the current liabilities in their definition of capital employed.

3. Long-term debt (or long-term liability).

   Note, however, that if the debentures are to be repaid within the next twelve months they would be shown as a current liability.

4. The authorized share capital should be shown as a note on the face of the balance sheet. It is there for reference/information purposes. It is not added to the issued share capital.

5. The ordinary shares.

   Note, however, that companies sometimes issue 'A' ordinary shares which do not have voting rights, and preference shareholders may have voting rights if their dividends are in arrear. The class rights do vary and to find out exactly what they are you must refer to the company's Memorandum and Articles of Association.

6. The ordinary shareholders. They are paid out last if their company has to be wound up.

7. The preference shares receive a fixed dividend.

   Note, however, that some preference shares may also have a right to participate in a distribution of profits (participating preference shares).

8. The nominal value of a share may also be referred to as the par value or the face value.

9. Share premium.

   Note that it is shown as a reserve in the balance sheet. It tends to be described as being a statutory reserve, because its use in the United Kingdom is governed/restricted by company law.

10. Revenue reserves represent ploughed back profits, i.e. retained or undistributed profits, which have accumulated since the formation of the company.

11. Revenue reserves are shown as liabilities because in most instances they are in effect amounts owing to the ordinary shareholders. They comprise amounts earned which could have been distributed to the ordinary shareholders.

12. The equity shareholders' interest in a company consists of the issued ordinary share capital paid up *plus* the reserves, i.e. both capital and revenue reserves.

13. Long-term debts consist of long-term loans, debentures and, if appropriate, the bank overdraft.

14. When it is used as a long-term source of funds. For example £5m secured on the fixed assets of a small company, which the company does not intend to repay for some considerable time, is perhaps better classified as long-term debt. It is most certainly not a current liability.

15. Fixed assets (and leasehold property) which we buy outright are shown in the balance sheet. Those which are rented are simply treated as an expense of the accounting period to which they relate, i.e. the rent is charged as an expense in the trading and profit and loss account.

16. Working capital equals current assets less current liabilities.
    Note that it is sometimes described as the circulating capital of the business.

17. Current liabilities.
    Note that the dividend proposed is an amount owing to the shareholders which will be paid within, say, the next six months.

18. A prepaid expense will be shown as a current asset.
    Note that it is, in fact, a type of deferred expense, i.e. something that was paid out during the current period, the benefit of which extends into the next accounting period. Thus a proportion of the expense will be consumed in the next (or a future) accounting period.

19. Calls are instalments of the balance of the amount owing from ordinary shareholders to the company on the shares which they hold. For example, £1 shares issued for £2.40, payable £1 now, the balance by two instalments of 70p each. Until the first of the 70p instalments is received the amount paid up is £1 per share and the calls amount to £1.40 per share. All of the calls received will be classed as share

premium i.e. £1.40 per share in excess of the normal (or par) value.

20. Capital reserves may be caused by:
    (a) share premium;
    (b) a revaluation of fixed assets;
    (c) the acquisition of shares in a subsidiary company;
    (d) the redemption of own shares.

The straight line method of depreciation
(Chapter 6)

1. £820 annual depreciation for fixtures and fittings.
2. £3,125 annual depreciation for office equipment.
3. £24,000 annual depreciation for plant and machinery.

The reducing balance method of depreciation
(Chapter 6)

Year 1   £2,000
Year 2   £1,500
Year 3   £1,125

The revaluation method of depreciation
(Chapter 6)

Year 1   £7
Year 2   £16

Port Peter plc (Chapter 7)

Port Peter plc trial balance

(1)				(2)	(3)
				+ or −	Balance
Destination	(Jumbled up) details	Debit £000	Credit £000	Adjustment £000	sheet effect £000
B/C	Authorized and issued £1 ordinary shares		400		
T	Sales		375	*Note* 4	
T	Purchases	140		Closing stock	
T	Stock 1 January 19X4	29		−20 T	20 CA
B/Res	Share premium		25		
P&L	Bad debts (written off)	3			
P&L	Wages and salaries	48			
B/FA	Motor vehicles (at cost)	40		*Note* 1	
−B/FA	Depreciation to date on motor vehicles		16	Depreciation 8 P&L	Depreciation to date
P&L	Motor expenses	9			−24 FA
				Note 2 Prepaid	(new cumulative)
P&L	Overhead expenses	30		−4 P&L	4CA
B/FA	Freehold land and buildings	437			
B/CA	Debtors	28			
B/CL	Creditors		23		
B/CA	Bank balance	32			
App	Profit and loss account		11		
B/LTD	10% debentures		50		
P&L	Directors' fees	56		*Note* 5	
−	Taxation	−	−	18 App	18 CL
B/FA	Fixtures, fittings and equipment (at cost)	80			
−B/FA	Depreciation to date on fixtures and fittings and equipment		30	*Note* 1 Depreciation 8 P&L	Depreciation to date −38 FA
B/CA	Provision for bad debts		2		(new cumulative)
		£932	£932		
	Proposed dividend			*Note* 3 App 30	30 CL

The note numbers in column (2) refer to the notes providing further information which was provided on pages 83–4 concerning the adjustments.

Chua Lim Ltd (Chapter 7)

Trading and profit (for internal reporting purposes) and loss account for the year ended 30 June 19X5

	£000	£000	£000
Sales			998
Less **Cost of sales:**			
Opening stock		94	
Add Purchases		700	
		794	
Less Closing stock		106	688
Gross profit			310
Add Discount received (i.e. non-trading income)			6
			316
Less **Expenses:**			
General expenses		15	
Salaries		104	
Discount allowed (i.e. an expense)		2	
Directors' fees		72	
Increase in provision for bad debts		4	
Debenture interest		10	
Telephone, stationery and printing		2	
Rates and insurance	5		
Less prepayment	1	4	
Audit fees		1	
Depreciation			
Plant and machinery	16		
Vehicles (40 − 16) × 25%	6	22	236
Net profit before tax			80
Appropriations:			
Less Corporation tax			25
Net profit after tax			55
Less Ordinary dividend (interim)		16	
Ordinary dividend proposed		20	36
			19
Add Balance b/f from last year			30
Balance c/f this year			£49

Balance sheet as at 30 June 19X5

Capital employed

	£000
Authorized share capital	
800,000 £1 ordinary shares	800

	£000	£000	£000
Issued share capital			
Ordinary shares			800
Reserves			
Share premium		80	
Retained earnings (P&L account balance)		49	129
			929
Long-term debt			
10% debentures			100
			1,029

Employment of capital	Cost	Depreciation to date	Net
	£000	£000	£000
Fixed assets			
Freehold land and buildings	850	Nil	850
Plant and machinery	160	52	108
Vehicles	40	22	18
	1,050	74	976
Working capital:			
Current assets			
Stock		106	
Debtors	85		
Less provision for bad debts (3 + 4)	7	78	
Prepayments	———	1	
Cash and bank balances		11	
		196	
Less			
Current liabilities (due within 12 months)			
Creditors	98		
Taxation	25		
Proposed dividend	20	143	53
			1,029

Comments

☐ The discount received represents the cash discount for the prompt settlement of amounts owing to creditors. It is non-trading income.

☐ The discount allowed is the cash discount which the company allows to their debtors for paying promptly and is therefore an expense.

☐ The provision for bad debts works in the same way as the provision for depreciation. This amount charged in the profit and loss account increases the cumulative of the provision which is often deducted from the debtors figure in the balance sheet.

☐ The debenture interest is charged in the profit and loss account; it is *not* an appropriation.

☐ The depreciation of the vehicles used the reducing balance method of depreciation, i.e. as a percentage of the cost in the first year and then as a percentage of the book value (cost less depreciation) from the second year onwards.

☐ The corporation tax charge is not simply a percentage of the net profit before tax. It has to be computed in accordance with tax law.

☐ Both the dividends paid and proposed go into the appropriation section of the profit and loss account, but only the proposed dividend, i.e. the amount which is outstanding, is shown as a current liability in the balance sheet.

☐ The balance carried forward in the profit and loss account of £49,000 is the figure which goes in the balance sheet reserves section as retained earnings (P&L account balance).

Iainwar Ltd (Chapter 8)

Funds flow

Sources	£000	£000
Share capital (£60 − £50)	10	
P&L account (£96 − £80)	16	
Long-term loans (£70 − £40)	30	
Depreciation:		
Plant and equipment (£38 − £28)	10	
Motor vehicles (£19 − £10)	9	
Creditors (£39 − £30)	9	84
Applications		
Freehold property (£135 − £105)	30	
Plant and equipment (£72 − £54)	18	
Motor vehicles (£32 − £20)	12	
Stock (£64 − £27)	37	
Debtors (£51 − £22)	29	126
Decrease in bank balance (10 + 32)		(£42)

The bank balance has gone down from £10,000 in 19X6 to an overdraft of £32,000 in 19X7, i.e. gone down by £42,000.

Emmsock plc (Chapter 8)

CASH FLOW STATEMENT FOR THE YEAR ENDED (FRS 1)
31 DECEMBER 19X7

		£000	£000
Net cash flow from operating activities	(W1)		80
Returns on investments, and the servicing of finance			
Dividends received		—	
Dividends paid		(15)	
Interest paid (given)		(22)	(37)
			43
Taxation			
Tax paid	(W2)		(11)
			32

Investing activities

Purchase of tangible fixed assets	(W3)	(65)	
Proceeds from sale of trade investments		—	(65)
			(33)

Financing

Proceeds from new share capital	(W4)	271	
Repayment of borrowings	(W5)	(225)	46
Increase in cash and cash equivalents			13

Workings and comments: **Emmsock plc**

W1 Net cash flow from operating activities

	£000	£000
Retained profit		25
Increase in general reserve		5
Depreciation: Plant and machinery	16	
Fixtures and fittings	7	23
Profit or loss on sale of fixed assets		nil
Interest paid on debentures and loans (given)		22
Tax appropriated		15
Dividend appropriated		20
		110
Increase in stocks	(6)*	
Increase in debtors	(13)	
Decrease in creditors	(11)	(30)
		80

*Increases in current assets mean that more cash flow is tied up and decreases in creditors means that cash flow has been used to reduce the amount outstanding. Thus, an increase in current assets and a decrease in creditors will both be deducted in computing the net cash flow from operating activities as illustrated per W1 above.

W2 Tax paid

	£000
19X6 Balance b/f	9
Add 19X7 appropriation (P&L A/c)	15
	24
Less 19X7 Balance c/f	13
therefore *Tax paid* =	11

The £11,000 was the actual tax paid during the year to 31 December 19X7, i.e. the actual cash paid to the tax authorities. Such fluctuations between the tax appropriated and tax paid over frequently happen in practice. This is caused by having to reach an agreement with the tax authorities as to how much tax has to be paid and changes in allowable expenditure/tax rates, etc.

W3 Purchase of tangible fixed assets:

	Cost £000
19X7	659
Less 19X6	594
	65

You can observe that this is made up of an increase in land and buildings of £50,000, an increase in plant and machinery of £10,000 and an increase in fixtures and fittings of £5,000. However, if the sale of any fixed assets had taken place during the year to 31 December 19X7, this would have had to be taken into account (see the section of Chapter 8 which covers this aspect).

W4 Proceeds from new share capital:

	Ordinary Shares £000	Preference Shares £000
19X7	400	50
Less 19X6	200	nil
	200	50
Total		250

In addition to the above, there was also the increase in share premium 19X6 £17,000 to 19X7 £38,000, i.e. an additional £21,000, making the total £271,000.

W5 Repayment of borrowings:

	Debentures £000	Loan £000
19X7	100	nil
Less 19X6	165	160
	(65)	(160)
Total		(225)

Note
You should appreciate that W1 above could all be computed by reference to the balance sheet. This was designed to help you when you are faced with the

situation of only being provided with the balance sheet. However, you were provided with the profit and loss appropriation account, and so should have been able to compute the figure much more quickly, as follows:

		£000
	Net profit before tax (given)	65
Add	Depreciation	23
	Interest paid	22
		110
Less	W1 increase in current assets and decrease in creditors	(30)
		80

Festiclyn (Chapter 8)

CASH FLOW STATEMENT FOR THE YEAR ENDED (FRS 1)
31 DECEMBER 19X8

		£000	£000
Net cash flow from operating activities	(W1)		77
Returns on investments, and the servicing of finance			
Dividends received		—	
Dividends paid	(W2)	(16)	
Interest paid	(given)	(5)	(21)
			56
Taxation			
Tax paid	(W3)		(58)
			(2)
Investing activities			
Purchase of tangible fixed assets	(W4)	(97)	
Sale of tangible fixed assets	(W5)	17	
Proceeds from sale of trade investments		—	(80)
			(82)
Financing			
Proceeds from new ordinary share capital		150	
New bank loan		60	
Repayment of preference shares		(120)	90
Increase in cash and cash equivalents			8

Workings   **Festiclyn plc**

W1 The net cash flow from operating activities:

	£000	£000
Net profit before tax (given)		109
Add loan interest (given)		5
= Net profit before interest and tax		114
Plus Depreciation (W4)	18	
Loss on sale of plant (W5)	3	21
		135
Less		
Increase in stock	(54)	
Increase in debtors	(8)	
Increase in creditors	4	
		(58)
		77

W2 Dividends paid:	£000	**W3 Tax paid:**	£000
19X7 b/f	16	19X7 b/f	64
Add appropriation	22		72
	38		136
Less 19X8 c/f	22	*Less* 19X8 c/f	78
Paid	16	**Paid**	58

W4 New plant and machinery purchased and the depreciation charge:

	Cost £000	Depreciation £000
19X7 b/f	490	76
Less asset sold	24	4
Balance 19X8 c/f (excluding new P&M)	466	72
19X8 c/f (including new P&M)	563	90
NEW PLANT & MACHINERY	= 97	= 18

W5 Sale of plant and machinery

	£000	£000
Sale proceeds		17
Less Cost of plant sold	24	
Less depreciation to date	4	20
LOSS ON SALE		(3)

Festiclyn plc (Working Capital)
SSAP 10 Funds flow
Statement of source and application of funds for the year ended 31 December 19X8

	£000	£000
Source of funds		
Net profit before tax		109
Adjustment for items not involving the movement of funds:		
(Add back) Depreciation (see 1), and	18	
Loss on sale of plant		
(Cost £24 – Dep £4) = £20 Net – Sold for £17 =	3	21
		130
Total generated from operations		
Plus		
Funds from other sources		
Ordinary shares	150	
Bank loan	60	
Sale proceeds from plant and machinery	17	227
		357
Less **Application of funds**		
Preference shares (repaid)	120	
Dividends (see calculation 2) paid	16	
Taxation paid (see calculation 3)	58	
New plant (see 1)	97	291
		£66

(1) Plant and machinery (£000) *Cost*		*Depreciation*	
Balance c/f (19X8)	490		76
Less Plant sold	24		4
	466		72
Balance c/f (19X8)	563		90
New plant	97	Depreciation (19X8)	18

Increase/(decrease) in working capital:

Stocks (75 − 21)	54
Debtors (27 − 19)	8
Creditors (increase in creditors = reduction in working capital) (25 − 29)	(4)

Movement in net liquid funds:

Bank (19 − 11)	8
	£66

Calculations required:	(2) *Dividends*	(3) *Taxation*
	£000	£000
	16	64
Balances b/f (19X7)	22	72
Add P&L account appropriations	—	—
	38	136
	22	78
Less Balances c/f (19X8)	—	—
	Paid (in 19X8) £16	**Paid** (in 19X8) £58

Thirstin Leas Ltd (Chapter 9)

1. Ordinary shareholders' interest = ordinary share capital plus reserves (i.e. £500 + £250 = £750 (£000s).

2. The working capital = current assets less current liabilities (i.e. £160 − £80) = £80 (£000s). (This was a recap from your studies of earlier chapters.)

3. Debenture interest = 10% × £150,000 = £15 (£000s). Provided that the whole amount had been issued before the start of the year, hence a full year's debenture interest.

4. Gross profit/sales:

$$\frac{\text{Gross profit}}{\text{Sales}} \times 100 = \frac{135}{500} \times 100 = 27\%$$

Because this was a manufacturing company, the manufacturing wages were treated as part of the cost of sales.

5. Net profit/sales:

$$\frac{\text{Net profit before tax}}{\text{Sales}} \times 100 = \frac{60}{500} \times 100 = 12\%$$

6. The acid test:

$$\frac{\text{Liquid assets}}{\text{Current liabilities}} = \frac{(160 - 50)}{80} = \frac{110}{80} = 1.375$$

7. Return on capital employed:

$$\frac{\text{Net profit before tax} + \text{debenture interest}}{\text{Capital employed}} \times 100$$

$$= \frac{60 + 15}{900} \text{ (as (3) above)} \times 100 = 8.34\%$$

8. Average collection period:

$$\frac{\text{Average debtors}}{\text{Sales}} = \frac{60 + 110}{2} = \frac{85}{500} \times 365 = 62 \text{ days}$$

9. Average credit period taken:

$$\frac{\text{Average creditors}}{\text{Purchases}} = \frac{35 + 65}{2} = \frac{50}{300} \times 365 = 61 \text{ days}$$

This was a nasty one! The purchases figure was available, i.e. £300, and so was used to give a more accurate picture.

10. Rate of stock turnover:

$$\text{Average stock} = \frac{40 + 50}{2} = 45 \qquad \frac{500}{45} = 11.12 \text{ times}$$

11. Sales to fixed assets:

$$\frac{500}{820} = 0.61$$

The manufacturing fixed assets were not available. To have used them rather than the total of all fixed assets would have provided us with a better indication of plant utilization.

12. The gearing:

$$\frac{\text{Debentures}}{\text{Capital employed}} = \frac{150}{900} \times 100 = 16.67\%$$

shows that 16.67% of the assets were financed from long-term sources, other than equity.

13. Interest cover:

$$\frac{\text{Net profit before tax} + \text{interest}}{\text{Interest}} = \frac{60 + 15}{15} = 5 \text{ times}$$

14. Two reasons why we could not compute certain investment ratios are as follows:

(a) The market price of the ordinary shares was not given.
(b) The net profit after tax was not given.

Also the paid/proposed ordinary dividend for the year was not given.

Woodcroft plc (Chapter 9)

Ratio analysis work sheet

Ratio	19X7	19X8	Brief comments
Liquidity: Current ratio			
$\dfrac{500}{400} : \dfrac{520}{380}$	1.25	1.37	Slight improvement. However could be on the low side when compared to industry figures.
Acid test (quick ratio)			
$\dfrac{300}{400} : \dfrac{340}{380}$	0.75	0.90	Improved in 19X8 to possibly around the industry average.
Profitability: Net profit to sales			
$\dfrac{120}{1200} \times 100 : \dfrac{180}{1600} \times 100$	10%	11.25%	Better margins, better control of overhead expenses = a better performance in 19X8.
Return on investment (return on assets)			
$\dfrac{120}{200} \times 100 : \dfrac{180}{260} \times 100$	60%	69.24%	Looks like a very good return indeed. Especially when compared to investing in a bank or building society.

Efficiency:
Average collection period

$$\frac{260+300}{2} = \frac{280}{1200} \times 365$$

$$:$$

$$\frac{300+340}{2} = \frac{320}{1600} \times 365$$ 86 days   73 days

An improvement in 19X8 in the credit control, i.e. collecting debts more speedily. However, if the industry average is say 60 days there is room for improvement.

Credit period taken

$$\frac{120+160}{2} = \frac{140}{1200} \times 365$$

$$:$$

$$\frac{160+180}{2} = \frac{170}{1600} \times 365$$ 43 days   39 days

Could be in the habit of paying off creditors too quickly. Many companies may take around 60 days or longer to pay their debts – paying the debts they owe in half the time they allow their customers!

(The purchases figure was not available so the sales figure was used.)

Stock turnover

$$\frac{160+200}{2} = 180 \text{ Average stock}$$

$$\frac{200+180}{2} = 190 \text{ Average stock}$$

Rate improved in 19X8 due to carrying a lower level of stock even though sales volume had increased.

$$\frac{1200}{180} : \frac{1600}{190}$$ 6.67 times   8.43 times

Investment:
Earnings/shareholders' equity

$$\frac{80}{200} \times 100 \quad \frac{130}{260} \times 100$$ 40%   50%   Looks like a high return.

Dividend cover

$$\frac{80}{60} \quad \frac{130}{70}$$ 1.34   1.86

Improving, but high payout could be a problem if the company has a bad year.

Earnings per ordinary share
(EPS)

$$\frac{80}{100} \qquad \frac{130}{100} \qquad \qquad 0.80 \qquad 1.30 \qquad \text{A high rate of return.}$$

Points to note (not part of the answer)

Without industry figures, it is quite difficult to make sound judgements. However, reasonable comments can be made by using the following general rules:

☐ The current ratio ought to be around 2.00.

☐ The acid test, i.e. one to one, ought to be around 1.00.

☐ The average collection period and period of credit ought to be around 60 days, which is quite typical.

☐ The profitability ratios can be compared to the cost of borrowing and/or the interest rates paid by banks and building societies.

☐ However, remember that ordinary shareholders received a two-fold return:

    (a) The earnings on their shares, some of which may be distributed to them as dividends, with the remainder being retained within the company, i.e. reinvested in the company.

    (b) The capital growth (or capital loss) on the shares which they hold.

However, to calculate just what return they are really getting is a difficult task, because of fluctuations in share prices.

Nether Ltd and Thong Ltd (Chapter 9)

Ratio analysis work sheet for year 19X8

Ratio	Nether Ltd	Thong Ltd	Industry average	Comments
Liquidity:				
Current ratio				Both below industry average, indicating possible liquidity problems.
$\dfrac{60}{40} : \dfrac{90}{60}$	1.5	1.5	2.00	

Acid test (quick ratio)

$$\frac{60-25}{40} \quad \frac{90-60}{60} \qquad 0.88 \qquad 0.50 \qquad 0.90$$

Thong Ltd does have liquidity problems, i.e. only 50p worth of liquid assets for every £1 owing in current liabilities.

Profitability:

Net profit before tax to sales

$$\frac{25}{125} \times 100 : \frac{40}{250} \times 100 \quad 20\% \qquad 16\% \qquad 20\%$$

Thong Ltd has a lower than average net profit margin. Possibly using the lower margin to attract a higher volume of sales.

Return on investment (return on assets)

$$\frac{25}{120} \times 100 :$$

$$20.84\% \qquad 26.67\% \qquad 24\%$$

$$\frac{40}{150} \times 100$$

Thong Ltd making more efficient use of its capital, i.e. making a better return on investment.

Efficiency:

Average collection period

$$\frac{20}{125} \times 365 : \frac{30}{250} \times 365 \quad \begin{array}{c} 59 \\ \text{days} \end{array} \quad \begin{array}{c} 44 \\ \text{days} \end{array} \quad \begin{array}{c} 60 \\ \text{days} \end{array}$$

Thong Ltd collecting its debts more quickly, i.e. more efficient credit control. Probably because it is desperate for cash.

(No average available – current year's figures used.)

Credit period taken

$$\frac{40}{125} \times 365 : \frac{35}{250} \times 365 \quad \begin{array}{c} 117 \\ \text{days} \end{array} \quad \begin{array}{c} 52 \\ \text{days} \end{array} \quad \begin{array}{c} 70 \\ \text{days} \end{array}$$

Nether Ltd taking too long to pay its creditors and Thong Ltd paying them too quickly. They are a source of short-term finance.

(The purchases figure was not available so the sales figure had to be used; also no average available so current year's figures used.)

Stock turnover

$$\frac{125}{25} \quad \frac{250}{60} \qquad \begin{array}{c} 5 \\ \text{times} \end{array} \quad \begin{array}{c} 4.17 \\ \text{times} \end{array} \quad \begin{array}{c} 7 \\ \text{times} \end{array}$$

Both on the low side possibly because they could be carrying too high levels of stock. Indicates the need for better inventory control.

Investment:
Earnings/shareholders' equity

$$\frac{20}{120} \times 100 \quad \frac{32}{150} \times 100 \quad 16.67\% \quad 21.34\% \quad 20\%$$

Nether Ltd not performing too well on these measures. This could have an effect on its share price.

Earnings per ordinary share

$$\frac{20}{100} : \frac{32}{100} \qquad 0.20 \quad 0.32 \quad £0.30$$

The stock turnover position for both companies suggests that stocks are moving too slowly through each company and that they may be carrying stock levels which are too high. This means that capital which could be available for other purposes is being tied up in stocks of raw materials, fuels, finished goods and work-in-progress.

It is recommended that the companies could adopt the following courses of action to improve their performance:

	Nether Ltd	Thong Ltd
Liquidity and efficiency	Reduce the stock level. (i.e. both to improve their inventory management, e.g. concentrate on getting rid of slow moving, low margin lines)	Reduce the stock level.
	Improve credit control (if Thong Ltd can do it, why can't Nether Ltd?).	Try to keep the credit control at this level, provided it does not involve giving hefty cash discounts for prompt payment.
	Reduce the time taken in paying creditors to around the industry average.	Take a little longer time to pay creditors, unless this means the loss of generous cash discounts for prompt payment.
Profitability and investment	Manage overheads more efficiently and increase gross margins (if possible).	Manage overheads more efficiently and improve gross margins (if possible).

Conclusions and recommendations

Nether Ltd is performing better than Thong Ltd when it comes to liquidity. However, Nether Ltd could experience some difficulty in meeting its obligations as they arise because it is working at a level which is below the industry average. Thong Ltd does have quite serious liquidity problems, as indicated by the acid test ratio. It has only 50p's worth of liquid assets for every £1 it owes to its current liabilities.

It would appear that Thong Ltd is achieving its higher volume of sales by working on a lower net profit to sales margin. Thong Ltd's profitability and investment performance is superior to Nether Ltd's, i.e. it is getting better returns on its capital employed and better returns for its shareholders.

Thong's very good performance on the average collection period is an indication that it has an efficient and effective system of credit control. However, when it comes to the period of credit taken from creditors, the figure (52 days) suggests that it could be paying its creditors too promptly. Nether Ltd appears to be taking far too long to pay its creditors, i.e. 117 days, compared to an industry average of 70 days. Thus, there is a possibility that creditors who feel that they are having to wait too long may take them to court. This could damage the company's reputation in the market place.

Comment (not part of the answer): You should be able to observe from your study of the figures, that profitability and liquidity do not go hand in hand. Although Thong Ltd is the more profitable, it does have liquidity problems.

Even where a ratio is satisfactory, i.e. around the industry average, this is no reason for inaction. If action can be taken to improve the performance, then it should be.

The problems of interfirm comparison (Chapter 9)

A comparison of the textile companies listed is difficult because:

1. Some of them may be highly diversified and others may not be.
2. Their product ranges could be significantly different.
3. Of the way in which the source data were arrived at, e.g. the application of the accounting concepts.
4. Of off-balance-sheet financing, e.g. some companies may be renting some of their plant, machinery and equipment.

5. Their year ends are different, i.e. the comparison does not cover the same accounting period/trading conditions!

6. As indicated by the turnover, the companies are different in size.

7. Some companies may have had certain fixed assets revalued, e.g. buildings, recently, some years ago, or never!

8. Some could be highly automated and others more labour intensive.

9. The net profit could be affected by location, e.g. the overheads of a company in South-East England compared to a company in North Wales could be significantly different.

10. The stock figures of certain companies could have been affected by window dressing, e.g. run down to a very low year-end level. This would enable them to show a higher rate of stock turnover.

Appendix 1

Internal final accounts – alternative formats

Profit and Loss Accounts[1]

	This year £000	This year £000	Last year £000	Last year £000
Sales		54,000		43,000
Cost of sales		36,000		34,000
Gross profit		18,000		9,000
Administration costs	3,000		2,000	
Selling costs	4,000		2,000	
Distribution costs	5,000	12,000	3,000	7,000
Operating profit		6,000		2,000
Interest payable		500		500
Profit before taxation		5,500		1,500
Taxation[2]		1,500		400
Profit after taxation		4,000		1,100
Dividends paid and proposed		1,600		800
Retained profit for the year		2,400		300

Notes
1. In this illustration the trading and profit and loss account is simply called the profit and loss account.
2. You should also note that, in practice, in the UK and certain other countries the tax figure is not a percentage of the profit before tax. It has to be computed in accordance with tax law e.g. certain expenditure may not be alllowed as a deduction for tax purposes, and taxation capital allowances for fixed assets would have to be computed.

Balance Sheet

	This year £000	This year £000	Last year £000	Last year £000
Tangible fixed assets		10,000		11,500
Current assets				
Stock	10,000		7,000	
Debtors	7,300		4,000	
Prepayments	400		800	
Cash at bank	600		900	
	18,300		12,700	
Creditors – amounts falling due within one year				
Trade creditors	3,800		4,000	
Proposed dividend	1,600		800	
Taxation	1,500		400	
	6,900	11,400	5,200	7,500
Total assets less current liabilities		21,400		19,000
Creditors – amounts falling due after more than one year				
10% Loan stock (20X4–20X7)		5,000		5,000
NET ASSETS APPLICABLE TO THE ORDINARY SHAREHOLDERS		£16,400		£14,000
Capital and reserves				
Called up share capital – ordinary shares of £1 authorised and fully paid		5,000		5,000
Profit and loss account (retained earnings)		11,400		9,000
Ordinary shareholders interest		£16,400		£14,000

The final accounts which are prepared for internal reporting purposes may follow a variety of formats. Each format is, however, a re-ordering/re-classification of the information contained in the accounting records.

The profit and loss account illustrated is in summary form and a more detailed analysis of each figure would no doubt be made available to appropriate personnel.

The balance sheet illustrated is designed to show the ordinary shareholders interest i.e. their 'equity', made up of ordinary share capital plus reserves, this year 16,400,000 and represented by the net assets applicable to their investment.

The heading, creditors – amounts falling due after more than one year, has been included in this format to make it more in line with the format used for external reporting purposes.

Index